The Promise of Hope

Finding Hope When You Face Challenges and Trials

Dave Haslam

The Promise of Hope: Finding Hope When You
Face Challenges and Trials

Dave Haslam
Cover design by Dave Haslam

Books > Non-fiction > Religion & Spirituality
Books > Non-fiction > Christian Books & Bibles
Books > Non-fiction > Mormonism

ISBN-10: 9798713005962

For Trisha, Logan, Maddy, Aiden and Colin.

You are my biggest reason for hope.

Table of Contents

Table of Contents

Preface

We live in a challenging world. There are so many people around us who are struggling. They go through each day feeling guilty, depressed or unworthy. There are many who want to obey the commandments and feel the blessings of the gospel in their lives, but despite their best efforts they constantly feel they are falling short. Sometimes I have felt that way. Maybe you have too.

Maybe you have experienced these feelings of frustration and sadness. Maybe you feel like the promises of the gospel can help other people return to our Heavenly Father, but that you are far too broken to ever become clean. You may feel condemned to fail this mortal test. Many people have these feelings and are left to wonder why a loving Heavenly Father would send them to this life if they are doomed to fail this mortal test. How can we believe the gospel is good news if it only makes us feel condemned? For some, these concerns cause them to feel constant doubt. These concerns rob them of the joy the gospel promises. For others, such questions lead them to completely give up their efforts to improve.

The good news of the gospel is that we are not condemned to failure. We are all imperfect and we will all stumble in our attempts to become like Jesus Christ. Our Heavenly Father knows us individually. He knows our weaknesses, but he also knows our potential. He loves us and he did not send us to this world to condemn us to failure. Through the plan of salvation and the Atonement of Jesus Christ, we all have the opportunity to overcome our weaknesses and become perfect. Our Father in Heaven sent us to mortality to succeed. As we understand the Atonement more fully and learn more about what we should expect in our journey back to our heavenly home, we can feel the joy of the gospel. We can have hope. It is my hope that this book can help you gain a deeper understanding of the gospel. That it can give you a greater reason to have hope in your life. I believe we not only have a reason to hope, but that through the gospel of Jesus Christ we have a promise of hope. It is my prayer that the ideas in this book will help you realize that promise in your own life and help you have hope in your journey back to our Heavenly Father.

The Golden Buddha

In the Wat Traimit Temple in Bangkok, Thailand sits a beautiful statue of Buddha. This statue is 10 feet tall, 10 feet wide and weighs five and a half tons.

It is made of solid gold. It is believed that the Golden Buddha was made sometime in the 13th or 14th centuries. The monks who created the Golden Buddha did so with extreme care and craftsmanship. It is not only an example of exquisite gold metalwork, but also cleverly engineered. The monks created the statue in nine pieces that smoothly fit together. It even has a key that allows it to be disassembled so it can be more easily moved. It is truly a marvelous work of art. This statue is one of a kind and while the value of the gold it contains is over 250 million dollars, its age and history make it a priceless treasure. But the true value of the Golden Buddha was not always so clear.

In 1767 the Burmese army invaded what is now Thailand. The army was destroying and looting all the temples they encountered. The monks expected the Burmese army would steal or destroy the Golden Buddha. To save the Golden Buddha, the monks covered it in stucco inlaid with pieces of colored glass to disguise its true value. Their trick worked and the invaders ignored the giant Buddha statue.

When the invaders left, the giant Buddha was left behind in the ruins of the temple. Eventually, all monks who knew about the true nature of the Golden Buddha died and with them the knowledge of the statue's true worth.

Sometime during the mid-1800s the statue was moved to Bangkok. Since it was believed the statue was just made of common stucco, it was thought to be of minimal significance, and it was placed in a minor temple. It stayed there without attracting attention or importance. It even spent over 20 years sitting under a simple tin roof because the temple did not have a building big enough to hold it.

All of that changed in 1955. The monks had constructed a larger building to house the ancient statue. They needed to move the Buddha statue into the new building. The workers did not have the benefits of heavy machinery and had to rely on ropes and pulleys to move the massive statue. As the workers labored to move the immense Buddha, one of the ropes snapped and the statue fell *hard*. It hit the ground hard enough that some stucco chipped off, revealing the shining gold that lay hidden beneath the rough exterior.

Work on moving the Buddha was immediately stopped. The workers started the laborious task of removing the stucco from the ancient statue. Bit by bit they carefully chipped away the stucco. Eventually, they were cleaning stucco out of ornate details and polishing the beautiful gold. At last, the beautiful Golden Buddha was now visible for all to see.

Today, the Golden Buddha is sought out by many who come to see the glorious statue. The Wat Traimit Temple where it resides has become a destination for believers and non-believers alike who all come to marvel at the Golden Buddha's beauty and craftsmanship.

You Are Golden

As you look at your life, you may feel that you are unimportant, of little worth, or too flawed to hope to make any real difference in the world. You may believe you are a giant stucco Buddha covered in cheap colored glass. When you feel this way—and I believe everyone feels this way sometimes—it is important to know that you are *not* alone. You are not insignificant. You are magnificent. You are not of little worth. You are precious and important in the world. You are not too flawed. You are a profound good preparing to be unleashed on the world. You are *not* a giant, stucco Buddha. You are a Golden Buddha.

This can be hard to believe when you are struggling with weaknesses and self-doubt. We all have those times when we feel the pain of our weaknesses. Each of us is often painfully aware of our weaknesses. These weaknesses can cause us to doubt our ability to be better. I am not going to try and tell you that you don't have weaknesses. Everyone has weaknesses. We are all Golden Buddhas that are still covered with a thick layer of stucco. To remove the layers of stucco that hold you back, you will need to do the work to remove them and reveal the gold within.

The good news is that everyone *can* improve. We can overcome our weaknesses and become the best versions of ourselves. To do this, you have to believe you can overcome your weaknesses and become what you have the potential to become. This point is important enough to be worth repeating. *You* have to believe *you* can overcome *your* weaknesses and become what *you* have the potential to become. This transformation requires hope and faith. You need to cultivate the hope and faith that you can become a Golden Buddha.

Hope and Faith

And if men come unto me, I will show unto them their weakness. I give unto men weakness that they may be humble; and my grace is sufficient for all men that humble themselves before me; for if they humble themselves before me, and have faith in me, then will I make weak things become strong unto them.

— Ether 12:27

When we are feeling weak and broken, it can be hard to believe that you can become better. You may want to have hope and faith but may feel it is difficult to have either. If you have felt this way, you are not alone. Many if not all of us, either feel this way now or have felt this way in the past. If we are to reach our true potential, we will have to overcome this doubt and find true hope and faith.

Hope and faith are skills and like other skills, hope and faith can be practiced, cultivated and strengthened. We can practice having hope. We can practice having faith. By its very nature practice implies doing something imperfectly at first. As you start to practice our hope and faith, you will have times you falter. You will have times when your hope and faith are weak or possibly fail you entirely. You will have times of frustration. But, just like anything else we practice, when we practice having hope and faith, over time our *ability* to have hope and faith will increase. You can build up your hope and faith muscles until they are strong.

The great news is that the Lord has promised us that when we humbly seek his help and rely on his grace, he will make weak things become strong in us. He will help us have hope and faith. He will help us overcome our weaknesses so the gold in us can shine.

Finding Your How

When your why is big enough, you will find your how.

— *Les Brown*

Most jobs in life can be accomplished in a variety of ways. However, it is always easier to complete a project successfully when you have the right tools.

When the monks discovered that the Golden Buddha was covered in stucco, they did not sit around and try to think the stucco away. And they didn't try to wash it off with water, peel it off with their hands or remove it with a jack hammer. Rather, they found and used the right tools.

While it is not recorded exactly what tools were used to remove the stucco from the Golden Buddha, we can imagine what this process might have looked like. Envision it in your mind now. Maybe you can see the monks carefully and methodically chipping away stucco with chisels and mallets. This would be a long and laborious process. Sometimes a large piece of stucco might pop off, but more regularly, small pieces are removed. Bit by bit, the magnificent golden statue becomes more and more visible. As more and more of the stucco is removed, you can imagine them starting to use small brushes and fine picks to clean stucco from the detailed gold work. Through this process, intricate patterns that were once rough and dirty and rough become brilliant and ornate.

Eventually, they start using rags and even finer brushes to polish the statue, now fully freed from its stucco shell until it shines gloriously for all to see. Surely, to complete their task, they found the *right* tools and used them systematically and consistently until the job was done.

Our individual quests to improve our lives and build stronger hope and faith are no different. Sometimes we will need to employ hammers and chisels as we make big and critical changes. At other times, we may need to focus on smaller but still critical changes with a fine pick. Wherever we are focusing our efforts, the right tools are critical, and the end goal is the same.

The purpose of this book is to explore ways each of us can build the hope and faith we need to create our greatest future. We need to learn what tools we have at our disposal in our efforts to improve and grow. We will discuss new perspectives that will help us see our weaknesses in a new light. We will also learn about tools we can each use to practice hope and faith in our daily lives. It is my hope and prayer that you will find these tools valuable in your daily efforts to chip away at the stucco covering your true self and reveal the glorious gold that is hidden inside you.

Understanding Imperfection

Even with all of the mistakes, opposition, and learning that accompany our mortal experience, God never loses sight of our eternal potential, even when we do. We can trust Him "because God wants his children back." And he has provided a way through the Atonement of His Son, Jesus Christ. The Atonement "is the core of the plan of salvation."

— Carole M. Stephens

The first tool we need to use to gain hope is an understanding of imperfection. Since we are all imperfect, it is important that we understand why. Why are we imperfect? Why would a loving Father in Heaven send us into this world and give us commandments that so readily highlight our imperfections? If we are to have hope that we can overcome our seemingly endless supply of imperfection, we need to understand what role our imperfections play in our efforts to improve. When we understand why it is acceptable, at least for now, that we are imperfect it opens our hearts to the hope that we can in time overcome our weaknesses.

Having Hope When You Are Imperfect

We fail to realize that mastery is not about perfection. It's about a process, a journey. The master is the one who stays on the path day after day, year after year. The master is the one who is willing to try, and fail, and try again, for as long as he or she lives.

— George Leonard

Let's start by getting one thing out of the way: we are all imperfect. Not only are we imperfect, but most of us are aware—usually painfully aware—of our imperfections. Despite our best intentions, each of us will make mistakes. We all make mistakes unintentionally by acting in ways that seem natural but that are not consistent with our best selves. At other times we choose to make mistakes intentionally. This happens when we know how the best version of ourselves would act but choose to do something else anyway. Whether intentional or unintentional, our mistakes can make us feel very inadequate. It can be difficult to know how to handle our feelings of inadequacy. After all, aren't we commanded to be perfect? Is that some sort of cruel joke?

Our loving Father in Heaven did not send us to Earth to feel guilty and doomed by our imperfections. We were not sent to this life to fail. We were sent here to learn and grow. If we are to learn how to have hope despite our imperfections, we need a better understanding of what it really means to be perfect.

We become perfect as we become like our Savior. This is something we all have the potential to do. Our goal is to gain his image in our countenance and have our hearts changed to be filled with his love (Alma 5:14, 19). We become perfect as we are filled with charity, which is the pure love of Christ (Moroni 7:47). But how do we do this? How can our hearts be filled with charity? How do we become like our Savior when we have so far to go? Becoming like the Savior will not happen instantly. It is a process. It will take time. We should not expect it to happen instantly. Because it is a gradual process, it is something everyone can do. Because it is a gradual process, we can all have hope when we feel imperfect. In this chapter we will talk about these ideas in more detail. We will try to understand how hope in the Savior can help us overcome the despair and guilt of our imperfections.

Parable of the Sacrament Prayer

(adapted from an original concept shared by Brad Wilcox)

It was a normal Sunday morning in a Sacrament meeting. The priests stood at the Sacrament table, breaking the bread for the Sacrament while the congregation sang a familiar reverent hymn.

As the last few notes from the organ sounded, the priests finished breaking the bread and stood reverently.

As the chapel fell silent, one priest knelt down to bless the bread. The priest confidently started repeating the Sacrament prayer he had recited many times before. He began, "O God, the Eternal Father, we ask thee, in the name of Jesus Christ…". Instantly, he realized he had messed up the prayer. Knowing the Sacrament prayer needed to be recited perfectly, he stopped. Feeling a little self-conscious, he looked over at the Bishop. The Bishop had noticed the error too and nodded at the priest.

The priest started the Sacrament prayer again. "O God, the Eternal Father, we ask thee, in the name of thy Son, Jesus Christ, to bless and sanctify this water." The priest froze again. He was blessing the bread. His face flushed red with embarrassment.

Doubts flooded into the priest's mind. How could he be having such a difficult time with this? What was wrong with him? Why couldn't he finish the same Sacrament prayer he had given correctly so many times before? He felt as if everyone in the congregation was staring at him. Judging him.

Out in the congregation, many sat with their heads bowed saying a silent prayer in their hearts for the priest. Many of them remembering the times they had made public mistakes, too.

The priest again looked over at the Bishop, more sheepishly than before. The Bishop looked back at the priest and gave a subtle nod of encouragement. The priest again bowed his head and began the Sacrament prayer. This time the priest made it almost to the end of the Sacrament prayer. He started to feel a little more relaxed and confident—and then he forgot another word near the end of the prayer and froze again.

Any relief or confidence he had started to feel instantly vanished. How could he have let himself mess up yet again? His previous thoughts of doubt rushed back into his head and weighed on his heart. Why couldn't he get even this simple thing right? Wasn't it obvious to everyone that he shouldn't be here? Why should he even keep trying when it was clear that all he would do was mess up, yet again? Why should he even bother trying?

Feeling a flood of self-doubt, he glanced over to the Bishop, convinced he would see nothing but a reproving look. The Bishop once again gave a soft smile and a nod of encouragement giving the priest courage to try one more time. On this attempt, the priest finished the prayer without error. Relieved, he looked one last time at the Bishop who gave an approving smile. The members of the congregation who had been praying for the priest smiled too as they gave a silent prayer of thanks.

As the Sacrament was passed, the Bishop smiled, knowing a lesson had been taught by a priest who only thought he was messing up. The Sacrament that day was not any less important or effectual because of the priest's mistakes. If anything, it was sanctified all the more by the repeated efforts of the priest to perform the ordinance perfectly.

Like the priest in this story, we all have times when we make mistakes and repent only to make the same mistakes again. Despite our best efforts, this is the nature of practice and growth. Yet, like the young man in this story, we have all been in similar situations where we have felt the guilt and self-doubt that inevitably accompany our failures. But we can learn several things that can help us see our failures from a different perspective.

Perfection Is a Commandment

God knows that you are not perfect, that you will fail at times. God loves you no less when you struggle than when you triumph.

— Dieter F. Uchtdorf

The first thing to remember is that we are commanded to be perfect by a loving Father in Heaven who knows we are not perfect. He knows you and me better than we know ourselves. He will not give us any commandments that are impossible for us to achieve. He will only give us commandments that will lead us to greater happiness. He does not expect us to be something we are not. Rather, he wants to remind us of what we have the potential to become.

"Be ye therefore perfect, even as your Father which is in heaven is perfect." (Matthew 5:48) is a commandment to strive continually to be like our Heavenly Father and our Savior, Jesus Christ. This commandment is especially important when we feel we have such a long way to go. We are all children of God. Just as a seed has the potential inside it to become a mighty tree and a caterpillar has the potential to become a beautiful butterfly, as children of the Almighty, we have within us the potential to become like him. We have within us the seeds of perfection. We each have within us the *potential* to become like him.

Understanding this truth helps us to see the commandment to be perfect for what it is: the loving encouragement of our Heavenly Father to His children.

God knows each of us individually. He knows you. Before you were born, you were taught at his feet in our heavenly home. He knows *you*. He knows your strengths and he knows your weaknesses. He knows you have the potential to become like him. Our Father in Heaven also knows we can only become perfect by improving one step at a time. The commandments are his loving guidance to help us in that journey.

When parents see their baby crawl or take those first unsure steps, they rejoice with their baby. Similarly, God loves us and rejoices every time we try to be a little better. Each time we choose to serve others or help lift someone who is down, we move one step closer to being like our Savior. We become a little more perfect. It can sometimes be hard to believe that these tiny steps can add up to anything significant, just as it is almost impossible to perceive the growth of a plant in a single day. However, as the tiny changes add up over time, it becomes easier to see the dramatic changes that occur.

You may have seen this if you have ever watched a time-lapse video of a plant growing. Usually, when we see plants, they look static. Sure, they may move when blown by the wind, and we can see that they change over time. Yet in the moment they don't appear to change very much. But when you see a time lapse recording of a plant, you quickly see just how dynamic they are. Flowers for example move to follow the sun. They grow and twirl. They dance. We are taught that "by small and simple things, great things are brought to pass" (Alma 37:6). We too can grow our perfection like a plant. We can follow the light of the Savior. We can grow. We can dance. We just have to realize that it will take time. But taking time doesn't diminish the value of the small and simple steps we make towards perfection.

You Are Imperfect, So Is Everyone Else

There is something interesting, almost paradoxical, about this path you've chosen: the only way for you to progress in your gospel adventure is to help others progress as well. To help others is the path of discipleship. Faith, hope, love, compassion, and service refine us as disciples.

— Dieter F. Uchtdorf

As we strive for perfection, it is easy to forget that every other person we encounter is also imperfect. Just like you, they are struggling along their own path to perfection. This can often be hard for us to believe because we often don't understand the struggles others are going through.

Henry B. Eyring once said, "When you meet someone, treat them as if they were in serious trouble, and you will be right more than half the time." Everyone is struggling with something. While some people are only struggling with minor things, many people are struggling with significant challenges. This is easier to believe if you remember your personal struggles. If you are like most people, you have probably personally experienced struggles, doubts, trials, pains, and heartaches. Many of us keep these challenges hidden from the world, but we all have trials and struggles. You have your personal challenges to overcome. So does everyone else.

No one is a finished product. As Dan Gilbert has said, "Human beings are works in progress that mistakenly think they're finished." Everyone is a work in progress. None of us are finished. This fact can be hard to accept, but it can also be a source of great hope. It can give us hope because if everyone is working through their personal imperfections, it means you are not alone in working through your imperfections.

This insight can help us each be more loving and compassionate to others when we see them in their moments of weakness and struggle. We can reach out to them with love and encouragement. When we do what we can to lift and encourage each other, we become more like our Savior. This is what Jesus did when he walked the earth. He lifted and helped those who were struggling. He healed the sick. He comforted the weary. He enlightened the confused and downtrodden. As we strive to follow the Savior's example of lifting and helping each other, we become more like him.

Practice Makes Perfect

That which we persist in doing becomes easier for us to do—not that the nature of the thing is changed, but that our power to do is increased.
— Ralph Waldo Emerson

We all have times we fail to live up to our desires to be like Christ. This imperfection despite our better desires is the precise reason for the Atonement of Jesus Christ. The Atonement allows us to reach our true potential. The blessing of the Atonement allows us to bridge the chasm between the imperfect people we are today and the redeemed and perfected children of our Heavenly Father we can eventually become.

Through the gift of repentance, we can all get back up and try again *every* time we fall. We are never beyond the hope provided by the Atonement of Jesus Christ. Satan knows this. He knows that each time we get back up after we stumble, we are a little better and a little stronger for it. And because he knows this, he has one goal: to make us believe we can't get back up and try again. Satan will do all he can convince you and I that we are not good enough. He does all he can to make us feel we have messed up too badly. He wants us to believe we are too imperfect for anyone to love. He wants to make us feel that we are too imperfect. He wants us to believe we are beyond hope. He knows if he can make us give up, he has won the battle for our souls.

Our Heavenly Father and Jesus Christ know our true potential. Because they know our potential, the Savior constantly and repeatedly invites each of us to "Come follow him." He knows that if we continue to try to follow him, we will eventually become like him. All we have to do is keep trying. All we have to do is get back up each and every time we fall.

Getting back up when we fall can be difficult. Striving to improve is work. It can be really hard work. Sometimes you may doubt your ability to get back up and try again. You may feel there is no point in continuing to try when your goal seems so far away. When this occurs, you can take comfort that your Heavenly Father loves you and he knows your true potential. As you seek the support of the Lord through the Holy Ghost, he will lift and strengthen you. He will help you have the hope and strength you need to stand back up and try again, regardless of how many times it takes.

It's All About Your Trajectory

Every one of us aspires to a more Christlike life than we often succeed in living. If we admit that honestly and are trying to improve, we are not hypocrites; we are human. If we persevere, then somewhere in eternity our refinement will be finished and complete—which is the New Testament meaning of perfection.

— Jeffrey R. Holland

Planes are off course over 90% of the time they are in the air. Pilots are still able to direct their aircraft to their desired destination by constantly adjusting the plane's course. Just like a plane flying a long distance, we may often find ourselves off course. If we fail to correct our course, these small deviations from the path of the gospel can cause us to arrive at an entirely different destination. But if we continually adjust our course, we too can arrive at our desired destination. Although each of us can start walking the path to perfection in this life, we should understand that attaining perfection will not occur for a long time. Like a ship at sea or an aircraft flying a long distance, we each regularly need to adjust our trajectory to stay on course. What really matters is not the daily adjustments you need to make but the direction you are headed. This does not mean that small decisions are unimportant. The small decisions allow us to stay on course.

An experience I had while serving as a missionary in Japan brought this lesson home for me. At the time I was serving in the city of Ichinomiya. Like many cities in central Japan, Ichinomiya had been severely bombed during World War II. After the war, the city was rebuilt with roads radiating from the train station in the middle of the city. I had always lived in towns where the roads followed a basic grid pattern. Because of this the layout of Ichino-miya was sometimes confusing.

One day, my companion and I were on our way to an appointment. The appointment was about a mile and a half away. We were riding our bikes along a road that was one street away from the road our destination was on. Being in a hurry and not wanting to take the time to wait for traffic lights, we decided to continue towards our appointment on the street we were currently on longer than we had planned. Eventually, we crossed the street and went over one block expecting to be at our destination. To our surprise, it was the wrong street. We looked at our map and realized the roads we thought were parallel, had branched away from each other some time ago. Although we had traveled a mile and half already, we still had over a mile to go in a different direction. What would have been a minor course correction for us earlier required a major adjustment later. From this experience I learned the importance of consulting a map and making timely course corrections.

In the scriptures, Alma teaches that "by small and simple things, great things are brought to pass" (Alma 37:6). The "small and simple" things are the things that help us adjust our course and allow us to keep heading in the right direction.

You Can Be Perfect in Small Things

Each family prayer, each episode of family scripture study, and each family home evening is a brushstroke on the canvas of our souls. No one event may appear to be very impressive or memorable. But just as the yellow and gold and brown strokes of paint complement each other and produce an impressive masterpiece, so our consistency in doing seemingly small things can lead to significant spiritual results.

—*David A. Bednar*

As we pay attention to the small and simple things in our life, we can ensure we are heading towards the right big things in our life. This requires us to make the necessary course corrections to keep ourselves on the path that leads us back to our Savior. Without these corrections, we run the risk of having the small errors we make derail us from achieving the great future our Heavenly Father has in store for us. Just like my experience so long ago on my mission, it is extremely easy for us to overlook how much the small deviations in our course in life can affect where we eventually end up. If we don't take notice of the small errors we make, we can't correct them. As we make such adjustments in our life, it is important to use our goal to be perfect like Christ as a guide. When we keep this goal in mind, we can use our small course corrections to stay on course.

While our road to complete perfection is surely a long one, it is important to understand that many commandments can be obeyed perfectly in this life. As we strive to follow the Savior's example and to obey the commandments, we are all like a young child learning to play a piano. When a child starts to learn the piano, they don't jump from being a new musician to immediately playing prestigious concerts. No one would expect this to happen. When you begin to play the piano, you start by learning extremely basic principles. How to hold your hands. Which keys play which notes. How to read music. How to count time. As a young student studies these and many more musical principles they slowly but surely start to build their knowledge, skill and ability to play the piano. They grow their ability little by little over time. The key to success in this effort is practice. By continuing to practice a piano student gains mastery. They eventually reach the point where they no longer need to think about how to hold their hands or which keys play which notes. This allows them to move on to more advanced concepts and give them the skill to play more challenging pieces of music.

As we each practice being more perfect, we are like the young piano student who is learning and mastering the fundamentals of playing the piano one at a time. As we practice the principles of the gospel, we can master them too. When we master principles of the gospel, they can become powerful tools we can use in our journey back to our Father in Heaven.

We can strive to obey many gospel principles perfectly. Paying tithing, keeping the Word of Wisdom, partaking of the Sacrament each Sunday, daily reading the scriptures, praying sincerely and many other commandments are in our power to do perfectly. You can know when you have paid a full and honest tithe. You can know when you are following the Word of Wisdom. Even commandments that are not as black and white as tithing and the Word of Wisdom can be mastered. We can learn to obey many of those commandments perfectly as well. I believe we are living a commandment perfectly when we no longer have to struggle to keep it. When it has become who we are. Maybe you have had this experience or know someone else who has. Someone who no longer has to *try* to care about their neighbors and serve them, but who naturally cares about their neighbors and serves them. Or someone who no longer has to *try* to find ways to share the gospel, but who openly shares the gospel with everyone. You see, the goal of the gospel is to make us like our Heavenly Father and Jesus Christ. To change our hearts to be like theirs. And when our hearts become like theirs in some of these ways, we are starting to perfect.

An ancient Chinese proverb says, "Before enlightenment, chop wood, carry water. After enlightenment, chop wood, carry water." We could say the same thing regarding perfection. Before perfection, chop wood, carry water. After perfection, chop wood, carry water. What does this mean? I believe it means that we often expect that somehow becoming like our Savior changes everything, that our life will be dramatically different than it is now. In some ways this is true. But I don't think our lives will change in the ways we might expect. Becoming more like Jesus Christ won't necessarily change how our lives look generally. Rather, becoming more Christlike changes *us*. Life will still go on. We will still need to chop wood and carry water. We will still need to serve others and follow the commandments. We still need to deal with challenges and problems. The thing that changes is that as we become more like our Heavenly Father and Jesus Christ, *how* we chop wood and carry water changes. *How* we serve others and follow the commandments changes. *How* we deal with challenges and problems changes. And this changes everything for us, even though we might still be chopping wood and carrying water.

Perfection Is a Gift

In this and every hour he is, with nail-scarred hands, extending to us that same grace, holding on to us and encouraging us, refusing to let us go until we are safely home in the embrace of Heavenly Parents. For such a perfect moment, I continue to strive, however clumsily. For such a perfect gift, I continue to give thanks, however inadequately.

—*Jeffrey R. Holland*

Continually practicing our ability to live the commandments will qualify you for additional help from the Holy Ghost. The Holy Ghost will give you the strength to persevere in your efforts to live the commandments that you personally find challenging. Our Heavenly Father wants us back. He, as the perfect example of a loving parent, wants to help us and will lead us and guide us home. When we do what we can to follow our Savior and partake of the blessings of the Atonement through repentance, he will help us to become more like him. He sends this guidance through promptings and impressions given by the Holy Ghost. He will send this guidance to us when we seek it. He will give us the gift of perfection as we practice being more Christlike.

Moroni taught, "Wherefore, my beloved brethren, pray unto the Father with all the energy of heart, that ye may be filled with this love, which he hath bestowed upon all who are true followers of his Son, Jesus Christ; that ye may become the sons of God; that when he shall appear we shall be like him, for we shall see him as he is; that we may have this hope; that we may be purified even as he is pure." (Moroni 7:48) As we strive to be like Jesus Christ and pray for his help, he will help us receive the gift of forgiveness and we will eventually become perfect even as he is perfect. He will *give* us his love in our hearts. He will change our hearts to be like his heart.

This is not a change we can make on our own but is a gift we are given as we do our best to keep the commandments. This is perhaps the greatest reason for hope. We don't have to make these changes on our own. We don't have to fight this fight alone. While we may not be perfect now, God has instilled in each of us the potential to be perfected through the Atonement of Jesus Christ. And he will help us get there.

Trust

Trust in the Lord with all thine heart; and lean not unto thine own understanding.

In all thy ways acknowledge him, and he shall direct thy paths.

—Proverbs 3:5-6

We have talked now about imperfection and how the Lord will help us overcome our weaknesses. When we start to have the hope that he will help us, we can then learn to trust in the Lord. As with any type of trust, trust in the Lord does not come instantly. Rather, we learn to trust in the Lord as we start to acknowledge his hand in our lives. This trust is also called faith and it will always help us recognize the many miracles that occur in our lives.

How to Create Miracles in Your Life

Wherefore, my beloved brethren, have miracles ceased because Christ hath ascended into heaven, and hath sat down on the right hand of God, to claim of the Father his rights of mercy which he hath upon the children of men?

For he hath answered the ends of the law, and he claimeth all those who have faith in him; and they who have faith in him will cleave unto every good thing; wherefore he advocateth the cause of the children of men; and he dwelleth eternally in the heavens.

And because he hath done this, my beloved brethren, have miracles ceased? Behold I say unto you, Nay; neither have angels ceased to minister unto the children of men.

—Moroni 7:27-29

Jesus Christ is a God of miracles. When we read the scriptures, we see account after account of the miracles he has performed. Some of these miracles, like healing the sick or feeding the multitudes or raising the dead were large and impressive. Other miracles that we read about are decidedly smaller and more personal. However, despite the range in magnitude of the miracles Jesus performed, each miracle was significant to the people who received it.

Throughout our lives and especially in times of trouble, we can find ourselves humbly searching for the Lord's help. Sometimes this humility is caused by our personal weaknesses and imperfections. Most everyone has had the experience of struggling with a weakness that they cannot seem to overcome on their own. They try and try and continually find themselves failing to improve. This can be a painful and frustrating experience. For many, these experiences cause them to throw their hands in the air and give up. They may think, "Why should I even try? I know I can't do it. I tried and I failed. Then I tried again, and I failed. This is just who I am." Have you ever felt this way? I know I have. When we have reached this point of realizing that we have many weaknesses we cannot overcome alone, it can humble us. It can help us understand why we need to rely on the Lord's help. At these times, we can be driven to our knees. We can feel the need to seek his help.

Weaknesses are not the only things in life that can motivate us to seek the Lord's help. Life is full of challenges. Some we create for ourselves. Some are created by the actions of others. Some of them are just part of the flow of everyday life. These challenges can also lead us to seek the Lord's help. They can prompt us to ask the Lord to perform miracles in our lives. Sometimes this help seems to arrive immediately and powerfully. But sometimes we may find ourselves waiting on the Lord. We may find ourselves wondering when he will send the help we so desperately need. It can be easy to feel like the Lord is holding back the miracles we long for. So, how do we see more miracles in our personal, everyday lives?

We can find many things we can each do to help us see more miracles in our lives. We will discuss three of the things that each and every one of us can do, today and every day, to start seeing more miracles. Those three things are being willing, having faith, and choosing to see.

We Must Be Willing

It has been said that this church does not necessarily attract great people but more often makes ordinary people great. Many nameless people with gifts equal only to five loaves and two small fishes magnify their callings and serve without attention or recognition, feeding literally thousands.

—James E. Faust

The miracle of the loaves and fishes is one of the many memorable miracles in the New Testament. The account is simple, Jesus was teaching a multitude of people and it came time for the people to eat and they were hungry. Jesus's disciples said that the multitude should go and buy food. Jesus saw that the people wanted to stay with him and continue to be taught the gospel. So, he said they did not need to go and commanded the disciples to give them food to eat. The disciples searched around and found that they only had five small barley loaves and two fishes, barely enough to feed themselves. As they looked at the multitude of over 5,000 people, they surely knew that they did not have nearly enough food to feed them all. How could the disciples possibly feed thousands of people with such a meager amount of food?

The disciples brought the five loaves and two fishes to Jesus. They offered him all they had. Jesus took their offering and blessed it and divided it into several baskets and commanded his disciples to take the baskets and feed the multitude. They trusted in his instructions and distributed the food to all those who were gathered to hear the teachings of Jesus. Each and every person who was gathered ate bread and fish from the baskets. When they had all eaten their fill, they gathered the baskets back together and found that they still had 12 full baskets of food left. The Lord had miraculously fed over 5,000 people from the humble offering his disciples and brought to him.

Many of us are called on to do great things in this life. We are given opportunities to serve in callings in our wards. In our homes we are called upon to raise children and to love and serve our families. In our communities we are instructed to be active forces for good, seeking to serve others, be examples to those around us and to share the gospel with everyone we meet. We may often feel that these responsibilities are completely outside our capabilities. When we feel this way, the challenges we are asked to face can make us feel inadequate. Like the Lord's disciples in the story of the loaves and fishes, the challenges we are given can make us ask, "What can we offer?" We can feel we are being asked to feed the multitude when all we have is a meager five loaves and two fishes.

When we feel this way, we can feel comfort as we remember that *we* don't have to magnify our efforts. When we put forth effort and do our best to do what the Lord asks us to do, *he* will magnify our efforts. We *can't* turn the five loaves and two fishes into enough to feed thousands. The Savior *can* turn our offerings, however small they may seem, into something that can bless everyone around us. We are asked to be willing to offer our talents and effort to the Lord. He can then magnify our talent and effort to accomplish his work. When we offer what we can to the Lord, he magnifies our efforts. He can turn our offering of five loaves and two fishes into a bountiful feast. He can use our offerings of time, talent and effort to produce miracles around us that are greater than we can comprehend.

For these miracles to happen, we must first make the offering. We must exert our effort. We must willingly give him what we can and trust that he can turn our offerings, however small, into something magnificent. The talent and ability we have to offer may not seem like much, but in the hands of the Master, they can lead to miracles.

We Must Have Trust

It isn't as bad as you sometimes think it is. It all works out. Don't worry. I say that to myself every morning. It all works out in the end. Put your trust in God, and move forward with faith and confidence in the future. The Lord will not forsake us. He will not forsake us. If we will put our trust in him, if we will pray to him, if we will live worthy of his blessings, He will hear our prayers.

—Gordon B. Hinckley

Another story, from the Book of Mormon, that also recently helped me understand more about miracles is the story of the brother of Jared. In this story, Jared and his brother were commanded by the Lord to flee from the Tower of Babel with their families and friends. The Lord led them through the wilderness for years on their way to a choice land. At one point in their journey, they came to the sea.

The Lord commanded them to build "barges" to cross the vast sea and continue their journey. These barges were not normal ships like one might imagine. We are told in the scriptures that they were "tight like unto a dish" and that they would be like "a whale in the midst of the sea." Rather than a normal ship, these barges were probably much more like a modern-day submarine.

Because the barges would be "as a whale in the midst of the sea," the Lord instructed that they should be built so they were tight like a dish and without windows to keep out water. These two requirements caused the brother of Jared to have two primary concerns about the vessels: how would they breathe inside the vessels and how would they see? Once Jared and his company finished constructing the vessels, the brother of Jared went to the Lord with these concerns.

> *And it came to pass that the brother of Jared cried unto the Lord, saying: O Lord, I have performed the work which thou hast commanded me, and I have made the barges according as thou hast directed me.*
>
> *And behold, O Lord, in them there is no light; whither shall we steer? And also we shall perish, for in them we cannot breathe, save it is the air which is in them; therefore we shall perish.*
>
> *—Ether 2:18-19*

The first thing I was impressed with as I studied this story was that the brother of Jared *finished* the vessels as he had been commanded *before* he went to the Lord to seek answers for his concerns.

Undoubtedly, the brother of Jared felt these concerns as he was working to build the barges. He could see some aspects of the Lord's instructions that seemed to have design flaws that would need to be fixed. Whether or not he thought the instructions from the Lord were flawed, he clearly had questions about various aspects of the barges. However, he did not let this stop him from following the commandments of the Lord. Instead, he did what he was commanded to do and when that was done, the Lord told him how to resolve his concerns.

We too may often see parts of the instructions we receive from the Lord that we don't fully understand. We may view some teachings as having flaws or inconsistencies. We may have questions. When this happens, do we stop and demand answers or do we move forward with faith and trust that the Lord knows what he is doing? Many people allow doubts to derail them from following the commandments and gaining the blessings of the Gospel. Questions can be hard to deal with and having faith and trusting the Lord can be a real challenge. It can be very hard to move forward with faith when we don't fully understand what the Lord has in store for us. But when we trust in the Lord despite our limited understanding, he can do more to perform miracles in our lives.

The brother of Jared showed his trust in the Lord by following the commandment to build barges even when he had questions about the Lord's instructions. The Lord knew what he needed the brother of Jared to do. When the brother of Jared and finished showing his faith by building the barges the Lord gave him answers about how to fix the issue of not being able to breathe in the barges. He instructed the brother of Jared to cut a hole in the top of the barges that could be opened to let in air, but then stopped up when it was necessary to keep water out.

The Lord did not answer all of the brother of Jared's questions, though. He told the brother of Jared to go and ponder and to find a solution to his question about how to light the vessels. The brother of Jared searched for a solution about how to light the vessels and he finally came up with an answer: *rocks*.

We Must Have Faith

After what was undoubtedly a great deal of soul-searching, the brother of Jared came before the Lord—perhaps hesitantly but not empty-handed. In a clearly apologetic tone, he said, "Now behold, O Lord, and do not be angry with thy servant because of his weakness before thee; … O Lord, look upon me in pity, and turn away thine anger from this thy people, and suffer not that they shall go forth across this raging deep in darkness; but behold these things which I have molten out of the rock," (Ether 3:2-3)

__Things__. The brother of Jared hardly knew what to call them. __Rocks__ undoubtedly did not sound very inspiring. Here, standing next to the Lord's magnificent handiwork, the impeccably *designed and marvelously unique seagoing barges, the brother of Jared offered for his contribution rocks. As he eyed the sleek ships the Lord had provided, it was a moment of genuine humility.*

—*Jeffrey R. Holland*

The brother of Jared had come up with a plan for providing light in the vessels they had built. He made some clear, glass-like rocks by melting down other rocks. Then he brought these to the Lord. He had faith that if the Lord touched the stones with his divine finger that the stones would glow and provide light in the barges as they crossed the sea. The Lord agreed to touch the stones and because of the brother of Jared's faith, he saw the finger of the Lord. The Lord then taught the brother of Jared that because his faith was so strong the Lord could not prevent him from seeing his finger.

When we approach the Lord with faith, we too can see miraculous things, but first we have to choose to have faith. Florence Shinn said, "Hope looks forward. Faith knows it has already received and acts accordingly." When we have faith, we do not only hope that something is true or believe that it can happen, we *act* as though it is true. Faith truly is a principle of action. When we let our faith lead us to action, it can become a powerful force in our lives. Faith will allow us to see many more miracles each and every day.

We Must Choose to See

> *Counting our blessings is far better than recounting our problems. No matter our situation, showing gratitude for our privileges is a fast-acting and long-lasting spiritual prescription.*
>
> *Does gratitude spare us from sorrow, sadness, grief, and pain? No, but it does soothe our feelings. It provides us with a greater perspective on the very purpose and joy of life.*
>
> *— Russell M. Nelson*

In November 2020, President Russell M. Nelson shared a powerful message with the world about the importance of expressing gratitude. As we all know, 2020 provided everyone with a seemingly endless stream of challenges and trials. During that year, many people experienced significant struggles. Many people lost jobs or had struggles with employment. Many have felt isolated and alone. Many missed opportunities and had to make significant adjustments to their lives. These trials were real, and they were genuinely hard. And for many they may have felt overwhelming. As the challenges continued to pile up through the year, it became easy to focus on everything that was going wrong. However, as President Nelson so wisely counseled, life is much better when we choose to focus on all the things we can be grateful for.

Despite the challenges that were encountered in 2020, I have many things I have been grateful for. I am grateful for the extra time I've had to connect with my family. I am grateful for the chance to focus more fully on my personal worship through better scripture study and family gospel discussions. I am grateful for the opportunity to disconnect from many of the distractions of my normal life and more fully focus on the truly important things. I am grateful for the chance to gain new insights into the worship practices that are of real value to me and my family and are not just part of our Church culture. I am grateful for a greater sense of the importance of the temple. I am grateful for these and many, many other things.

When we choose to view our blessings with gratitude, we can begin to see just how active the Lord is our lives. We can start to see the miracles that constantly happen around us. These miracles have always been there, but we have to choose to see them. Once we've seen them, we can learn from them and find ways to carry those lessons with us into the future.

> *Men and women who turn their lives over to God will discover that he can make a lot more out of their lives than they can. He will deepen their joys, expand their vision, quicken their minds, strengthen their muscles, lift their spirits, multiply their blessings, increase their opportunities,*

comfort their souls, raise up friends, and pour out peace.

— Ezra Taft Benson

Our Heavenly Father and Jesus Christ know each of us personally. They know you by name. They are playing an active role in each of our lives. When we trust in them and have faith, we can more fully gain their help in every aspect of our lives. When we choose to have gratitude and see the many blessings that surround us, we can start to see how the Lord is leading and guiding our lives. We can start to see many more miracles in our lives, because the miracles are there. They are already happening. We just have to open our eyes to see them. It is my hope that we can all have this gratitude in our daily lives.

Finding Joy When Times Are Tough

We are all living in interesting and challenging times. Like everyone else in the world, we have felt the effects of the COVID-19 epidemic in our home and community. Many people who have become sick. Many people are unemployed. Some people are truly struggling with difficult challenges to make it from day to day. At this time, our thoughts and prayers go out to all those who are experiencing the effects of this pandemic in profound ways.

We also see many people who are reaching out to their neighbors. Many who are lifting those who are down and working to help those in need.

Regardless of what trials you are experiencing in your life, know that you are not alone. Trials are a part of life that everyone will experience. We can each come to understand many truths that can help us make it through our trials. In this section, I will share some thoughts I have been having as my family has experienced challenges. I do not presume to have the answers for why we have trials. It is my hope that the things that have helped me may also help you as you work to adapt to the challenges we are all facing.

Trust the Lord Knows What He Is Doing

Sixty-odd years ago I was on a farm in Canada. I went out one morning and found a currant bush that was at least six feet high. I knew that it was going all to wood. There was no sign of blossom or of fruit. So I got my pruning shears and went to work on that currant bush, and I clipped it and cut it and cut it down until there was nothing left but a little clump of stumps.

As I looked at this little clump of stumps, there seemed to be a tear on each one, and I said,

"What's the matter, currant bush? What are you crying about?"

And I thought I heard that currant bush speak. It seemed to say, "How could you do this to me? I was making such wonderful growth. I was almost as large as the fruit tree and the shade tree, and now you have cut me down. And all in the garden will look upon me with contempt and pity. How could you do it? I thought you were the gardener here."

I said, "Look, little currant bush, I am the gardener here, and I know what I want you to be. If I let you go the way you want to go, you will never amount to anything. But someday, when you are laden with fruit, you are going to think back and say, 'Thank you, Mr. Gardener, for cutting me down, for loving me enough to hurt me.'"

— Hugh B. Brown

We may not always understand why we are called on to endure the obstacles and challenges we encounter. We may feel that we are being punished or picked on. However, we can come to trust that these experiences are being given to us by a loving Heavenly Father to help us become more like him. He gives us challenges and obstacles to help us reach our true potential. He knows what we can become. The Lord is the Gardener. He has a plan for us and will put us where he needs us to be. Part of my experience as a missionary helped me to come to understand that the Lord will put us where we need to be when we are willing to let him guide us.

On my mission I had the unique opportunity to have four mission presidents. My mission presidents were President Mackley, President Diamond, President Shimizu, and President Evans. These men were great spiritual leaders. They each sought the guidance of the Lord and helped us all become better missionaries. While they were all very spiritual men, they all brought different experiences to their role as mission president. They each guided us in a slightly different direction as a mission. Through the experience of having these four great men as mission presidents, I learned that the Lord can do his own work. I learned that he will put us where he needs us to be.

My first mission president, President Mackley was always teaching us that we should constantly be inviting everyone to be baptized. Whenever new missionaries arrived in the mission field, he always had everyone sing the hymn "Who's on the Lord's Side, Who" in the morning devotional on their first morning in Japan. He was a fearless man and he helped us be fearless in our efforts to spread the gospel. This led to a lot of action. We were focused and we worked very hard.

At about the halfway point of my mission, President Mackley finished his time as mission president. He was replaced by a new mission president, President Diamond. President Diamond was a very disciplined man.

He was also very different from President Mackley. I remember thinking at the time that it would be interesting to see how things would be different with a new mission president. It was exciting to have the opportunity to learn from two mission presidents as a missionary. In our first zone conference with President Diamond, he taught us to use the power of the Book of Mormon in every aspect of our missionary efforts. He encouraged us to seek wisdom in its pages and he taught us to use the spiritual power of the Book of Mormon to bring others to Jesus Christ.

Not too long after he joined us, however, President Diamond became ill and had to return home. It all happened so suddenly. One day, President Diamond was there and the next day he was gone. This surprised us all. At the time, President Shimizu just happened to be returning home from being the mission president at the Tokyo Mission Training Center. He and his wife were visiting family, who lived in our mission. He was asked if they would be willing to take a little detour on their way home to allow him to serve as interim mission president until President Diamond could return. President Shimizu agreed to step in as our mission president while President Diamond recovered.

President Shimizu was also a great man. He knew about missionary work and the history of missionary work in Japan. You see, he had been one of the missionaries who had originally opened our mission. His wife had also been a missionary in those early years of missionary work in Japan. The thing he taught us the most was to have faith in the work. Have faith in the message of the gospel and in our power to bring it to the people of Japan.

This was a timely message. You see, at the time, Japan was not an area where we saw a lot of people accept the gospel. It was often considered a "hard" mission. I remember being in a training meeting with President Shimizu and several branch presidencies. One of the branch presidents broke down over his frustration at trying to grow their branch. Their branch was tiny. They only had about six members who attended regularly. I still remember the testimony that President Shimizu bore to everyone that night. When he was a young missionary, he and his companion had been the first missionaries to open the area where this tiny branch was located. They were the pioneering missionaries who started to share the gospel in that area. President Shimizu told us about how they had prayed to be led to people who were ready to receive the gospel. Then they had gone out with his companion with the express goal of finding someone to teach who could be a branch president. He taught us about showing true faith in the Lord and then putting that faith into action.

Eventually, the word came that President Diamond wouldn't be returning to the mission. President Shimizu would stay until a new mission president could be called.

While we were all very sad to hear that President Diamond wouldn't be returning, we were grateful for the time we had to work with and learn from President Shimizu and his wonderful wife. My last mission president was President Evans. I only had the opportunity to work with President Evans for a couple of months. He was full of vision and the Spirit. Those last months of my mission were great. My companion and I gave away dozens of Book of Mormons. We had more lesson appointments than I had had at any other time in my mission. We were excited and saw the work of the Lord rushing forward.

Through this experience I was able to see the hand of the Lord at work. At none of these times did I feel that any of my mission presidents were doing anything incorrect. They were all led by the Spirit and did their best to fulfill their callings. They each steered our mission in subtle but distinct ways. It felt like the Lord was picking up our mission from one path and gently, but firmly placing it on another. Each mission president filled their role in this change and in the end, the mission was where the Lord needed it to be. Many years later I had lunch with my last companion and heard his stories about the great spiritual blessings and success that were seen in the mission as it moved forward on the path the Lord had chosen. As we seek to trust the Lord and follow his commandments, we too can come to see his guiding hand in our lives. He will place us where he needs us to be so we can accomplish the work he needs us to do. This is a profound blessing, and it begins with trust.

The Lord is at the helm. This is the Lord's church. This is the Lord's work. We are all his children. When times of trial come, it is natural to feel the fear of uncertainty. We can trust that the Lord is in charge. He is doing what he needs to do to put us where he needs us to be. As I have seen all the changes that occurred in 2020 due to the COVID-19 pandemic, I can't help but feel that the Lord is trying to put us where we need to be. The changes in the world that have come about due to the 2020 COVID-19 pandemic, and other changes that come from other trials we experience are there to help us. To me, these changes feel a lot like the changes that occurred during my mission. When we are enduring our trials and experiences, it can help to remember that the Lord knows what he is doing. It may be that the Lord is trying to move us collectively and individually from the path we were on to place us more firmly on his path. We can all have faith that the Lord is at the helm. This is the Lord's work, and it will not be frustrated.

> *Yes, you face challenges. But so does every generation. These are our days, and we need to be faithful, not faithless. I testify that the Lord knows about our challenges, and he is preparing us to meet them.*
>
> *— Stephen W. Owen*

We are living in challenging times. It is likely that our challenges will continue. May we each trust in the Lord. He is truly at the helm. He is guiding his church and will be active in each of our lives if we will let him. It is my hope and prayer that we can each have faith and trust in the Lord. It is my faith that as we show our trust in the Lord, he will help us learn and grow through all our trials. He will put us on the path that will lead us back to him.

Vision

Cultivate an attitude of happiness. Cultivate a spirit of optimism. Walk with faith, rejoicing in the beauties of nature, in the goodness of those you love, in the testimony which you carry in your heart concerning things divine.

The Lord's plan is a plan of happiness. The way will be lighter, the worries will be fewer, the confrontations will be less difficult if we cultivate a spirit of happiness.

— Gordon B. Hinckley

As we begin to trust in the Lord, he will lead us in our journey through life. We can rely on his guidance to give us a vision of the wonderful future we have in store. Just as the Lord has led Lehi and Nephi, the brother of Jared, Moses and the Israelites and countless others in their journeys to promised lands, so too will he lead us in our journey home to him.

Our Journey Through the Wilderness

I am not afraid of storms, for I am learning how to sail my ship.

— Louisa May Alcott

Don't believe in miracles — depend on them.

— Lawrence J. Peter

At the beginning of the Book of Mormon, we are told the story of the prophet Lehi and his family. Lehi had seen a vision and prophesied to the Jews at Jerusalem that they would be destroyed if they did not repent. The unbelieving Jews hated Lehi because of his prophecies and many of them started to plan to murder Lehi. Lehi was warned by an angel in a dream that people were going to kill him and that he should take his family and flee into the wilderness. Lehi obeyed. At the time, Lehi had four sons Laman, Lemuel, Nephi, and Sam. As the story unfolds, we learn how these four sons reacted to the trials and challenges that accompanied their journeys in the wilderness. Laman and Lemuel often found fault with their father and others. They resisted the guidance he gave and complained about the challenges they faced. Nephi believed his father and trusted in the Lord. He had faith and appears to have always done his best to have faith and obey the commandments he was given. Sam trusted in the testimonies his father and his brother Nephi.

As we read the first two books of Nephi, it is easy to feel impressed by Nephi's faith and diligence. He always seems to approach every problem with faith and optimism. Laman and Lemuel provide such a stark contrast to Nephi that we often only view them as the villains in Nephi's heroic story. When we do this, we miss the real story of Laman and Lemuel. Their story is a cautionary tale we all need to understand. Let's face it, most of us are often a lot more like Laman and Lemuel than we probably want to admit. Most of us struggle to keep at least some commandments. Many of us are often tempted to complain or compare ourselves with others. For most of us, faith often doesn't come as easily as it seems to have come for Nephi. While we often talk about how we should be like Nephi, most of us are probably more like Laman and Lemuel.

Both Laman and Lemuel had the gospel in their lives, cared for their families, and often did what the prophet asked them to do. They had trials and challenges and questions and doubts. They had frustrations and conflicts. Nephi also experienced many of the same challenges. He lived through the same trials. In the end, however, Laman and Lemuel and their descendants fell into darkness and disbelief while Nephi and his descendants continued to be blessed by the gospel. What made the difference? What did Laman and Lemuel not do that led them to losing the blessings of the gospel? What did

Nephi do that led him to gaining the blessings of the gospel? How can we follow Nephi's example so that we can be blessed in our trials and challenges?

One of the primary differences in how Laman and Lemuel and Nephi approached their challenges is in their vision of where they were going and how they would get there. Each of these brothers viewed their journey in very different ways. During their journey, Lehi's family encountered many challenges and obstacles. They were commanded to return to Jerusalem to retrieve the brass plates after weeks of traveling in the wilderness. They were commanded to return to Jerusalem a second time to convince Ishmael and his family to join Lehi's family in their journey. They struggled traveling through the wilderness for years. They toiled. At times they struggled to find food and nearly starved. Eventually, they were commanded to build a ship to cross the ocean.

In all of these experiences, Nephi started with his basic trust in the prophecies of his father and the words of the scriptures. He knew that he could "go and do the things which the Lord hath commanded, for he knew that the Lord giveth no commandments unto the children of men, save he shall prepare a way for them that they may accomplish the thing which he commandeth them." (1 Nephi 3:7). He sought the guidance of the Lord through the prophet when his family was suffering for the want of food (1 Nephi 16:18-31). He fearlessly approached the seemingly insurmountable task of building a ship to cross the ocean (1 Nephi 17:7-9). Nephi knew the Lord was guiding him to the Promised Land and he never lost sight of where he was going. He was looking forward to the future the Lord had promised. He had hope. He had faith. And this faith gave him the determination to face every trial. To him the trials were all just steps on the path to the Promised Land.

Laman and Lemuel, on the other hand, consistently viewed their obstacles from the perspective of what they felt they had lost instead of what they stood to gain. When they lost their family's wealth to Laban, they were angry. When they struggled in the wilderness, they longed for their more comfortable life back in Jerusalem. When they had difficulty understanding the prophecies of their father, they complained that the Lord wouldn't help them understand. When they were told to help build a ship, they mocked Nephi because of the size of the task. Repeatedly, they viewed every obstacle as insurmountable and complained at the difficulty of the path that was before them. They constantly looked back at their past and mourned what they felt they had lost. They did not trust in the Lord. Despite having seen angels and repeatedly hearing the voice of the Lord, they did not have sustaining hope or faith. They did not trust that the Lord had something greater in store for them, so they were always looking backwards, wishing for the life they'd had before leaving Jerusalem.

As we study these different reactions to difficulties, it can teach us about ourselves and how we can better handle the trials we will encounter in our *wilderness*. The Lord knows our potential and he knows our struggles. He has given us the stories about Laman and Lemuel in the Book of Mormon because they teach us things we need to know. We can learn several important lessons from Laman and Lemuel.

The Two Wolves

An old Cherokee is teaching his grandson about life. "A fight is going on inside me," he said to the boy. "It is a terrible fight and it is between two wolves. One is evil—he is anger, envy, sorrow, regret, greed, arrogance, self-pity, guilt, resentment, inferiority, lies, false pride, superiority, and ego."

He continued, "The other is good—he is joy, peace, love, hope, serenity, humility, kindness, benevolence, empathy, generosity, truth, compassion, and faith. The same fight is going on inside you—and inside every other person, too."

The grandson thought about it for a minute and then asked his grandfather, "Which wolf will win?"

The old Cherokee simply replied, "The one you feed."

— Native American Parable

I believe this Native American parable gets at the heart of the story of Laman and Lemuel. Before we talk about the lessons we can learn from Lehi's eldest sons, we should understand more about who Laman and Lemuel were and try to put their lives in context.

Laman and Lemuel were the sons of a prosperous and respected man. While we don't know Lehi's profession, we are told that he was wealthy. As the eldest son, Laman stood to inherit his father's fortune and take over his role in the community. He had a bright future ahead of him full of respect in the community and comfort in his home life. Lemuel was likely also in a position to step into a life of prominence because of his father. We can trust that, just like Nephi, Laman and Lemuel were "taught somewhat in all the learning of *their* father" (1 Nephi 1:1). They were not destined for lives of toil and hard labor but for lives of prominence and respect. We also know from Nephi's account that Laman and Lemuel had been taught the gospel, the history of the Israelite nation, and the teachings of the prophets. They knew of the Lord and his dealings with Israel. They knew of their people's covenants and commandments and customs. They had great parents who had done their best to pave the way for their children to have a bright and wonderful future.

From this we can see that Laman and Lemuel had vast amounts of opportunity in their lives. They surely had ambitions and hopes for the future. They had plans and expectations and that all disappeared when Lehi was commanded to take his family and flee into the wilderness. This was a sudden change of circumstance and we see throughout Nephi's account that Laman and Lemuel had a really difficult time understanding why they had to abandon their former lives. While they had been taught about the Lord and the gospel, their hopes didn't always align with the plan that God had for them. We too may find ourselves in this situation. We may find that the Lord has plans for us that we don't understand. When we do, we may be tempted to react in the same way as Laman and Lemuel, with complaining and frustration. By understanding how they chose to react, we can learn how to choose a better way when we encounter our personal trials.

Our Attitude Matters

Cultivate an attitude of happiness. Cultivate a spirit of optimism. Walk with faith, rejoicing in the beauties of nature, in the goodness of those you love, in the testimony which you carry in your heart concerning things divine.

The Lord's plan is a plan of happiness. The way will be lighter, the worries will be fewer, the confrontations will be less difficult if we cultivate a spirit of happiness.

— Gordon B. Hinckley

In every aspect of life, our attitude matters. The way we choose to view the world dramatically affects the experiences we have. When we approach our problems with optimism, gratitude and happiness then every experience can help us to become more like our Savior. The philosopher Anaïs Nin said, "We see the world not as it is, but as we are." We will *always* view our experience through the lens of our attitude. The good news is we can choose the attitude we want to adopt. Your attitude, and therefore the effect of your experiences, is a choice you get to make. As you choose your attitude, you get to decide what kind of world you want to live in.

We see this very clearly in the story of Laman and Lemuel. One consistent element in their story is that Laman and Lemuel were always quick to assume the worst. Whether trying to get the brass plates from Laban, hunting for food, learning from their father, or building a ship, they often approached challenges with pessimism. In these situations, they always focused on the negative and, because of this, their challenges were always difficult obstacles that brought frustration and suffering into their lives.

It is easy to understand Laman and Lemuel's attitude given the scale and scope of the things they were commanded to do. We may often feel the same way as we approach the challenges we encounter in our lives. It is worth taking a moment to consider how you choose to face the experiences that happen in your life. How do you respond to the challenges and commandments you receive? How do you feel when life trips you up or you encounter trials and obstacles? How do you view the other challenges and heartaches you experience? For example, do you complain about how hard it is to share the gospel? How do you feel about ministering? Do you find joy in your study of the Book of Mormon and in temple attendance? How do you feel when things just aren't going your way? If I answer these questions honestly, I have a lot I can do to improve. Maybe you do, too.

The good news is that we can all greatly improve how we experience our trials and challenges. You see, our trials and challenges are not objective things. They are not inherently good or bad. They just *are*. They become *good* or *bad* only as we assign meaning to them. We choose the meaning of our experiences and challenges by how we choose to view them. Wayne Dyer is quoted as saying, "If you change the way you look at things, the things you look at change." As we change the way we look at our trials and challenges our trials and challenges change. We can see this in action in many areas of our lives. Is work or school a frustrating chore or an open opportunity? Is an illness a punishment or a humbling trial that helps us build our faith? Is serving other people a burden or a wonderful chance to emulate the Savior? Is Sabbath and temple worship an obligation or a special blessing that allows us to feel our Heavenly Father's love? We get to decide the answer to these and many other questions as we choose how we will view our experiences.

This pattern is one we see repeatedly in the account of Lehi's family on their journey to the promised land. The many challenges and trials Lehi's family experienced were endured by all of them. Laman, Lemuel, Sam and Nephi were *all* sent to retrieve the brass plates. They were *all* involved in hunting for food. They *all* journeyed and toiled in the wilderness with their young families. They *all* helped build a ship. They *all* showed their faith by climbing on the ship they built. And they *all* trusted the Lord to lead them safely over the ocean. Yet, they did not all have the same growth in faith and righteousness through these experiences. Nephi chose to view these experiences as a path to the promised land and his faith grew. Laman and Lemuel chose to view these experiences as merely trials and hardships. They blamed their father whom they called a "fool." The resulting effect on their spiritual growth was profound in that they eventually fell away from the gospel. The key difference was how they *chose* to view their experiences. Their attitude was everything.

What does this mean to us? It means that our attitude is the single greatest determiner of how our experiences, both good and bad, will affect us. The great news is that our attitude is something we can practice and control. No one can make you pessimistic. No one can make you doubtful. Likewise, no one can make you optimistic and no one can make you exercise faith. These are all things we must choose for ourselves. We each have the power to choose how we interpret and react to the experiences that come our way. This choice may be hard, but you do have a choice. You may feel that you are naturally inclined to react in a particular way and your day-to-day experiences may reinforce this opinion. You may find yourself constantly reacting to your challenges with frustration and doubt. This does not mean that you are naturally pessimistic. Rather it means you have built a habit of pessimism. The good news is that we can cultivate an attitude of optimism and faith. You can practice this new attitude until it becomes your default. These changes may be difficult and will often take time, but they are something everyone can do. Changing habits is often very challenging because it is easiest to continue doing what you already do by default. As you work to change that default over time, you can replace it with a new, better default. This is the promise of the Gospel of Jesus Christ that we can all change. We can all turn from the natural man to find a better way. We can all become more like our Savior. He is there to help us change and become better. When we face the challenges we inevitably encounter in life with faith and optimism, we open ourselves to receive the Lord's help and guidance. The Lord is truly a God of miracles. When we choose to trust him and move forward in faith, we allow ourselves to see more miracles in our lives.

We Must Be Personally Converted

A person may get converted in a moment, miraculously. But that is not the way it happens with most people. With most people, conversion— spiritual rebirth and the accompanying remission of sins—is a process; and it goes step by step, degree by degree, level by level, from a lower state to a higher, from grace to grace, until the time that the individual is wholly turned to the cause of righteousness. Now this means that an individual overcomes one sin today and another sin tomorrow. He perfects his life in one field now, and in another field later on. And the conversion process goes on until it is completed, until we become, literally, as the Book of Mormon says, saints of God instead of natural men.

— Bruce R. McConkie

I have always been fascinated by the relationships between natural laws and spiritual laws. One such relationship I find very insightful is the Law of Inertia or Newton's First Law of Motion. The Law of Inertia states that an object will stay in its current state unless acted upon by external forces. A billiard ball remains stationary until it collides with another ball. A speeding car will continue moving until the driver applies the brakes. When something is small or moving very slowly, it doesn't take a lot of effort to stop it. But when something is massive or moving very fast, it can take an immense amount of force to slow it down or change its direction. It is easy to see how this law plays out in the physical world that surrounds us. We can see it at play as we interact daily with the physical world. But I believe this law is just as applicable in other areas of our lives. Just as the physical objects around us obey the Law of Inertia, the spiritual aspects of our lives also obey this law.

In a spiritual sense, we are all *objects in motion*. We all have spiritual momentum. Each of us learn line upon line and we grow or shrink by degrees. We build or destroy this spiritual momentum bit by bit with each and every decision we make. Day by day and decision by decision we are either increasing or decreasing our spiritual momentum. Depending on the decisions we have made in the past, future decisions can be either really easy or really challenging. Each time you pray, read scriptures, ponder truth, take the Sacrament, attend the temple or reach out to another in love, you add positive spiritual momentum. Likewise, each time you willingly choose not to follow the gospel, maybe you choose to gossip or shirk a church assignment or avoid reading your scriptures or praying, you remove some spiritual momentum. This spiritual momentum increases or decreases over time depending on how your decisions affect it. A large boulder doesn't stop easily and when you build significant spiritual momentum, living the gospel becomes much easier to do.

Laman and Lemuel provide examples of this principle in action. Throughout the story of their lives, we can see how they consistently made decisions that dropped their spiritual momentum. For each time they tried to live the gospel and follow the commandments, we are told that they also harbored vast amounts of resentment and doubt. They continually, or at very least regularly, let these resentments and doubts become the focus of their attention. Like a misaligned wheel or a boat dragging an anchor, these complaints and doubts provided constant opposition to their spiritual growth.

Maybe you have experienced this in your life. I know I have. Too often we let our complaints, frustrations, perceived offenses, jealousies, grudges, and misunderstandings become the focus of our attention. When we allow such feelings to become our focus, it stops us from focusing on the things that will help us grow. Often this obscured focus is the result of pain we feel. We may be hurt when someone does something like excluding us from activities or making choices we don't agree with. Maybe someone has a personality that we find offensive or acts in a way we find frustrating. Maybe they fail to fulfill their responsibilities and we feel we have to pick up the slack. Maybe they seem to have things easy when we are experiencing hardships. Maybe we feel hurt because of something someone said or how they have treated us. Regardless of the reasons for our hurt of frustration, when we focus on our hurt feelings, complaints, grudges, and frustrations it prevents us from fully embracing the gospel and following the Lord. The opposite of this is also true. Each time we choose to have faith, to forgive others, and to rely humbly on the Lord we break free from a weight that is holding us back. We must do this if we desire to build true spiritual momentum and become the men and women the Lord needs us to be.

As I have mentioned before, this can be *really* difficult. We should remember that we are working to overcome the natural man. The feelings we experience come naturally and often may seem to come automatically. Despite our natural inclinations, our reactions to the events of our lives can be trained and guided. We do have a choice in how we react to our experiences. If we want to overcome the feelings that come naturally and to become like our Savior, we need his help. To become truly like Jesus Christ is not something we can do on our own. As we learn to rely on the grace and mercy of Jesus Christ, he can replace our natural reactions with higher and holier reactions. He can change us from the "natural" men and women we are to the holier men and women we can become. This requires us to become personally converted to the gospel of Jesus Christ. It requires us to choose a better way and do our best to follow the Savior. One step at a time we can choose to strengthen our better selves until we become like Jesus Christ and our very natures are changed to be like him.

Small and Simple Things Are Super Important

My beloved associates, far more of us need to awake and arouse our faculties to an awareness of the great everlasting truths of the gospel of Jesus Christ. Each of us can do a little better than we have been doing. We can be a little more kind. We can be a little more merciful. We can be a little more forgiving. We can put behind us our weaknesses of the past, and go forth with new energy and increased resolution to improve the world about us, in our homes, in our places of employment, in our social activities. May we go with determination to try a little harder to be a little better.

— Gordon B. Hinckley

When we think about becoming converted, we are talking about **choice**. In life we can always choose how we will react to the events we experience. Regardless of the circumstances we may find ourselves in, we can always choose our reactions. We can choose to be happy and optimistic or choose to be sad and frustrated. We can choose to approach challenges with hope and faith, or we can choose to approach them with bitterness and despair. But we can always choose. We have agency.

Agency is the ability to choose. This ability to choose is a privilege the Lord has given each of us. Agency is important because without us choosing to follow the gospel, we can never become like our Heavenly Father. Becoming like him is not something that can be forced upon us, it must be pursued and willingly accepted. In fact, before we came to this life, we were all involved in a great war in heaven that centered on this principle of choice.

In the scriptures and through modern revelation, we are taught about this war. In this great war, we were given the option of two plans for our mortal test here in this life. The first plan was that we would be sent to this world with the opportunity to prove ourselves. We would have choice and we would be given the opportunity to repent. We knew that this plan would require us to choose and that we would stumble and struggle along the way. The second plan was proposed by Lucifer. His plan was that we should come to this world, but we would be compelled to follow the gospel "that one soul shall not be lost" (Moses 4:1). Lucifer proposed that he would guarantee that we would all return to our Heavenly Father, but his plan would require us to forfeit our agency. Knowing that we cannot truly become like our Father in Heaven without using our agency, our loving Heavenly Father chose the first plan. This ignited a huge war of ideologies that ended in Lucifer and one third of the children of our Heavenly Father's spirit children losing the opportunity to come to this world and get bodies. They lost the opportunity to prove themselves and continue to grow. For everyone that has lived or will live in this world, we chose that we would do our best to follow the gospel and so we could become like our Father in Heaven. The fact that you are here in this life is testament to the choice you made in the pre-earth life. Each of us knew and believed in the importance of agency and chose to follow the Lord's proposed plan. In the pre-earth life, each of us had hope and faith that we could successfully progress to become like our Heavenly Parents through the choices we would make in this life.

If agency is so important to our mortal experience, then we should strive to understand what agency is. Many people get confused by different definitions for agency. Some people refer to agency as *free agency*. They act as if we can freely choose anything including that we should also be free to choose the effects of our actions. They believe that regardless of our choices we should be allowed to be happy and have joy without experiencing any consequences. The agency we have been given in this life is not *free agency*, it is *moral agency*. *Moral agency* allows us to choose our actions. We can choose what we will do and how we will react to the events of our lives. But while we can choose what we will *do*, we are not always able to choose the *outcome* or *consequences* of our choices. While we have the choice of how we will act and react, the consequences of these choices are dictated by the laws of God. If we are to gain true peace and joy and happiness and become perfect like our Heavenly Father, we must choose to follow his laws and commandments.

Having this gift of agency does not mean we immediately know how to use it properly. We all come into this world as natural men and women. We all come into this world as beings who are not yet like our Father in Heaven. In the scriptures, this state is called *the natural man*. We all experience natural feelings and reactions to the events of our lives. We are undisciplined, we get frustrated, we react in anger, we make mistakes, and we are selfish. This is a state we all experience in different ways and which we must all strive to overcome. The miracle of the gospel is that we can learn and grow and overcome our natural tendencies. The Lord has given us commandments as guideposts to help us know who we can become and what we need to do to become like him. He will help us change for the better. He will help us reach our true potential as sons and daughters of loving Heavenly Parents. We have the power to do this as we rely on the Lord and consistently do the small and simple things of the gospel. The true hope of the gospel and the Plan of Salvation is that we don't need to change from our fallen imperfect selves immediately, but that we can grow and learn over time. We can overcome our weaknesses step by step, continually improving a little more each day until we truly become like our Father in Heaven. As President Gordon B. Hinckley taught us, each day we can "try a little harder to be a little better."

To "try a little harder to be a little better," we must start by consistently doing our best to do the seemingly small things that keep us firmly on the gospel path. We must do the little things like praying, studying the scriptures, attending church and partaking of the Sacrament. As the story of Laman and Lemuel unfolds, we learn that they didn't do these small things and it led to dramatic effects in their lives. When they didn't understand their father's revelations, they did not seek guidance in prayer. Rather they complained that the Lord didn't help them understand. While we don't know exactly what the daily lives of Laman and Lemuel were like, it is easy to believe that they treated many of the small and simple things of the gospel casually. It seems they did not do the small and simple things that we learn about as small children in Primary. Perhaps they didn't pray regularly or sincerely. Perhaps they did not search the scriptures and ponder on the truths found there. Perhaps they just went through the motions of worshipping the Lord without letting the truths of the gospel sink deeper into their hearts. Because of this casual approach to the gospel, they did not build the strong testimonies they needed to get them through their trials with their faith intact. They still had to endure the trials, but they ended up in a very different place spiritually.

So how can we learn from their experience as we "try a little harder to be a little better"? One thing we must do is sincerely strive to do the small and simple things. Are we humbly striving to pray from the heart to do we just say prayers? Are we striving to feast upon the words of Christ, or do we only read the scriptures? Do we serve others out of obligation or do we serve them out of love? Do we make the Sabbath a special day to reflect and focus on the Lord or do we treat it as just another day to relax and play? Answering these and other similar questions can help us know where we need to try a little harder in our lives so that we can be a little better every day.

We Need to Look at the Bigger Picture

If we have a love of God and know his goodness, we will trust him, even when we are puzzled or perplexed.

Thus Laman and Lemuel did not understand the relationship of mortals with God, and, worse still, they did not really want to understand. They sought to keep their distance from God. Furthermore, being intellectually lazy, they did not count their blessings, when gratitude could have lessened the distance. But it was never inventory time for Laman and Lemuel.

— Neal A. Maxwell

One thing that I find difficult to wrap my head around is the concept of eternity and the scope of the gospel plan. It is even difficult to know how to approach such concepts. Even when I try to ponder just the scope of everything in my life, it is almost impossible to comprehend. I can comprehend that we have a Heavenly Father who does know all things. I know that he has a plan for each of us and when we put our faith and trust in him, he will help us know what we should do. Having this faith allows me to gain a small but important glimpse of what the gospel is truly about and why it is important. This helps me put the daily struggles and challenges I face into perspective. This faith is a guide when making important decisions. It helps me to be better. My faith is not perfect. I still have times of doubt and times when I struggle. But, as I do my best to show faith in the Lord, the Lord helps to reinforce my faith. This kind of faith is a powerful blessing available to each and every one of us as we seek to follow the gospel and place our hope and trust in our Heavenly Father and Jesus Christ.

Our faith in the gospel becomes stunted when we choose to focus too closely on our immediate trials and challenges. When we focus too closely on our current challenges, we lose sight of the bigger picture of the gospel. Often what we perceive as a giant boulder is nothing more than a pebble we are examining too closely. When we do our best to take a step back and look at the bigger picture of life and the gospel plan, the Lord will help us gain a clearer view of the trials we experience. Viewing our trials and challenges with the proper perspective can help us see them more clearly and allow us to approach them with more hope and faith.

Without proper perspective our faith and hope can become weakened. This happens when we fixate on the problems and challenges we encounter instead of seeking the Lord's help.

In Nephi's account, we see this happen repeatedly to Laman and Lemuel. They often became focused on their problems and lost sight of the bigger plans the Lord had for them. When they were commanded to return to Jerusalem and retrieve the brass plates, they did not focus on what blessings the record on the brass plates would bring into their lives. Instead, they focused on the length and difficulty of the journey back to Jerusalem and the challenges they would have convincing Laban to turn over the brass plates. When they toiled in the wilderness, they focused on their hardships and not on the Lord's promise to lead them to a promised land. They did not have a clear vision of the bigger picture and this kept them from understanding what the Lord had in store for them. It hindered their hope and faith. Because they never fully developed the spiritual strength they needed, Nephi was told he would become a ruler and a teacher over them. Their focus on the disappointment and anger they felt at not being chosen to rule the people drove them to try and kill Nephi multiple times. Laman and Lemuel's lack of hope and faith in the Lord eventually led them to fall away from the gospel path and lose the blessings the Lord had prepared for them.

We can also see this same outcome in the lives of many people in our modern world. It is easy to become so focused on one challenge or one trial that we lose sight of everything else. Some even choose to forfeit the blessings available to them in the gospel because they focus on a single doubt, question, point of doctrine, or personal trial. We will all have times when we have doubts, questions, or don't fully understand what the Lord has commanded us to do. We will all also have times when we will experience trials and challenges that we don't fully understand. These experiences will test the limits of our faith. It is critical in these times that we do not lose our hope and faith in the bigger vision of the gospel. What does the gospel mean to you when viewed in the context of your entire life? What can the gospel mean to you and your family in the eternities? When we approach our doubts, questions and challenges with the greater perspective we get from the gospel, we can gain and maintain the hope and faith we need to overcome our trials and learn and grow from them. They can become blessings that bring us closer to our Heavenly Father and strengthen us spiritually.

Life is hard and full of challenges. Sometimes the challenges are minor bumps in the road. Sometimes they are really, really hard. We must do our best to remember what we learn from Laman and Lemuel when we face these challenges. We can each choose how we will approach our trials. As we continue to have hope and trust in the Lord, we can build our spiritual strength line upon line. We can feed that good wolf and starve the evil wolf. We can become the spiritually powerful men and women our Heavenly Father intends for us to be.

The Lord loves each of us. I truly believe that he sends us challenges in life that will help us grow and learn. He is helping us to become like him and our challenges will help us do that if we let them. Remember the Lord has given us tools to help us in these times of trial. The gift of the Holy Ghost, the scriptures, modern prophets and the Atonement all enable us to learn and grow every day. As we continue on our journey of life, we can trust in the promises of the Lord. We can take hope and know that just like Laman and Lemuel and Nephi, the Lord is guiding each of us to our own *land of promise*. Trusting in the Lord's guidance will make all the hardships of our journey worthwhile. When we view the journey as a blessing from our Heavenly Father our trials can strengthen our faith.

How to Be Guided by Vision

You are not alone on this journey. Your Heavenly Father knows you. Even when no one else hears you, He hears you. When you rejoice in righteousness, He rejoices with you. When you are beset with trial, He grieves with you.

Heavenly Father's interest in you does not depend on how rich or beautiful or healthy or smart you are. He sees you not as the world sees you; He sees who you really are. He looks on your heart. And He loves you because you are His child.

Seek him earnestly, and you will find him.
— Dieter F. Uchtdorf

As we have discussed through the stories of Nephi, Laman and Lemuel, having a vision of where you are going in life can powerfully influence what we achieve and who we become. We are all on a journey to a "land of promise." We have all been promised through the teachings of the prophets that if we follow the commandments in this life, we will inherit the mansions of our Father in Heaven when this mortal life is over. This is a wonderful promise and I do have faith that it will be our reward if we do our best to live the gospel. But sometimes it can be hard to remember our ultimate goal when we are experiencing the day-to-day struggles and problems we encounter as part of our journey. The promise of a place in our Father's kingdom can often feel too far away to provide us with any sense of purpose.

Because our personal land of promise seems so far away, it can be helpful to find ways to remind us of this vision. We can learn truths that will help us remember that we are on a journey to our very own land of promise. Some things that can help us in this journey back to our heavenly home include reading the scriptures, attending the temple, and envisioning your future. Each of these practices can help us maintain our hope and perspective.

Reading the Scriptures

When we want to speak to God, we pray. And when we want him to speak to us, we search the scriptures.

— *Robert D. Hales*

When Lehi was journeying in the wilderness, he awoke one morning to find a strange object sitting outside his tent. This object was a gift from the Lord and was called the Liahona. The Liahona was a marvelous device the Lord prepared to guide Lehi's family through the wilderness. We are told in the Book of Mormon that the Liahona had writing on it and "pointers" like a compass. Nephi recorded this about the Liahona: "the pointers which were in the ball, that they did work according to the faith and diligence and heed which we did give unto them. And there was also written upon them a new writing, which was plain to be read, which did give us understanding concerning the ways of the Lord; and it was written and changed from time to time, according to the faith and diligence which we gave unto it. And thus we see that by small means the Lord can bring about great things." (1 Nephi 16:28-29) The Liahona worked as Lehi and his family had faith. When they were faithful, the Liahona gave guidance and direction specific to the needs of Lehi's family. It gave them guidance and directed them on their journey through the wilderness. It led them to wild game when they needed to feed their families, and it showed them how to steer their ship when they crossed the ocean to the promised land. But it only worked when they had faith.

The Lord has given each of us with an equally marvelous tool to guide us in our journey through life. The scriptures are our Liahona. Just as the Liahona in Nephi's account worked by faith, the scriptures will also work according to our faith and diligence. When we sincerely study the scriptures in faith, they will guide us safely through this life. For the scriptures to guide us in this way requires us to read them in faith trusting that the Lord will guide us.

Attending the Temple

And I, Nephi, did go into the mount oft, and I did pray oft unto the Lord; wherefore the Lord showed unto me great things.

— 1 Nephi 18:3

Another thing we learn from Nephi's account is the importance of going to holy places to converse with the Lord. In ancient times, prophets were often commanded to go to the mountains to converse with the Lord. Moses, Enoch, Nephi, and many other prophets were directed to go to the mountains when they needed to commune with the Lord. For them the mountains were sacred places where the Lord could talk to His servants.

In our time, we too can go to the "mount of the Lord's house" when we worship in the temple. The temple truly is a place where we can go to draw nearer to the Lord and feast upon the blessings of the Spirit. The temple is a place that can help us remember that, as the Jesuit Priest Pierre Teilhard de Chardin observed, "We are not human beings having a spiritual experience. We are spiritual beings having a human experience." Regularly visiting the temple can give each of us a vast increase of spiritual strength to help us endure the challenges of life.

Envisioning Your Future

Who you want to be in the future is more important than who you are now, and should actually inform who you are now. Your intended future self should direct your current identity and personality far more than your former self does.

— Dr. Benjamin Hardy

Your vision of where or who you want to be is the greatest asset you have. Without having a goal, it's difficult to score.

— Paul Arden

Nephi was a great example of what we can do with our lives when we allow the vision of our future to motivate us and guide us through our trials. Regardless of what obstacles and struggles he encountered; Nephi always kept his focus on his vision of the promised land. This vision and his hope in the Lord's promises gave him the strength to overcome every adversity with faith.

We can follow Nephi's example by keeping in our minds the vision of what the Lord has promised us. One of the best ways I have found to do this is by imagining ourselves as we can become with the Lord's help. Despite where you may be in your life now—despite the challenges, weaknesses and shortcomings you feel—the Lord has promised each of us that we can become perfect through the Atonement. The miracle of the gospel of Jesus Christ is that we can all become so much more than we are now. We can become clean. We can become holy. We can become *like* our Heavenly Father and Jesus Christ.

One exercise that can help us to gain this vision of our potential future is to imagine what it would be like to meet and talk with your future self. What would the future you say? What advice would they have for you now? What are they like? How do they live? What is important to them? Try to imagine every detail of the encounter and hold on to that vision of yourself and allow it to help guide you now. As you do this, you can seek the Lord's guidance and He will help you to see His vision for your future. He will help you to understand who you have the potential to become.

I recently did this exercise myself and this is what I imagined.

The Interview

I am sitting in the chapel of the temple waiting to attend a session with my family. As I wait for my wife, our children and their spouses, a man walks up and sits next to me. "Hello. Do you mind if I join you?" he asks. I look up and see a face that looks instantly familiar and at the same time completely foreign. I feel I know this person and at the same time I can tell by looking in his eyes that I have never met him before.

"Sure," I say, gesturing to the seat next to me.

"Isn't it wonderful to be in the House of the Lord?" he asks. Before I can answer, he continues, "It always seems to me the things we learn while in the Lord's house are not only the most important, but also the simplest."

I nod in quiet agreement and look up again into that face that is both familiar and unknown. He smiles, chuckles a little then says, "You don't know who I am yet, do you?"

"I'm sorry," I stammer, "but no. I know that I know you from somewhere, but I can't quite put my finger on it."

He smiles a warm, friendly smile and chuckles again. I can tell from his smile and his warm, comforting gaze that he truly cares for me. I also get the feeling that his gaze and smile are always this warm for everyone he meets, but that doesn't make them any less endearing. "You can't *remember where we've met because we haven't met before. Or, more correctly, you haven't met me before. I know all about you, though. I know your hopes and dreams, your fears and doubts. I know things about you that you don't even know yet."*

"—How?" I manage to get out. "How do you know so much about me if we haven't met before?"

He smiles again and continues, "You misunderstood. I said you haven't met me before. I have met you, though. I have seen through your eyes because I am you. I am the version of yourself that you have the potential to become. I am your future."

"How is that possible?" I blurt out incredulously as I look up again and see his eyes fixed on mine. But even before I finish asking the question, I know that however impossible or strange it may seem, this man sitting next to me is me.

"Don't worry about that for now. I don't know that a simple explanation would make sense anyhow. And besides, how is not the important question right now, 'why?' is the question you should be asking."

"Okay, then, why are you here?", I ask absently, my mind racing.

"Well, that one I can try to answer. You see, there are many reasons why I could be here. But the most important reason, though, is to help you understand the vast potential within you that you have not yet tapped into. You see, as you already believe, you and everyone else has a vast potential lying dormant within them. God has placed that potential within each of us and commanded us to use it. He has commanded us to do all we can to learn and grow and to lift and serve others. And He expects us to do just that. The unfortunate thing is that so few people ever discover their full potential. They get distracted by every shiny object they encounter or discouraged by every little bump in their path. They let what they call 'life' get in the way of their dreams and end up living unspectacular lives of mediocrity and dullness."

"Occasionally, God lets some people see through the fog of life to catch a glimpse of a future that may be. That is why I am here to talk to you today."

He stops talking for a moment to give me a chance to process what he had said so far. Raising an eyebrow inquisitively, I ask, "But why me?"

He smiles again. "That doesn't really matter. What does matter is that since it is you, what will you learn?" He gives a half chuckle, "I hope you *take this opportunity to understand what the Lord has in store for you and what He is hoping and expecting you to become."*

"Okay," I stammer, "then can I ask you a question?"

"Sure," he answers, "what would you like to know?"

"Everything, I guess," I exclaim, louder than intended, "I mean, I barely know what I want my future to be, let alone what to expect. What do I need to know? What can you tell me?" I look down at the floor starting to grasp the implications of the situation.

"Well, don't get too far ahead of yourself. For starters, the first thing you need to know is that you are never going to know the answer to those questions. I know you don't know the answers for yourself now. I don't know the answers to those questions for myself either. You see, the Lord never intended for us to know exactly where we are going in life. He designed this life to force us— no, to allow us—to walk by faith. He expects us to think things through, pray for His guidance and then to take a step into the dark, not knowing exactly where our feet will land. When we seek His guidance and move forward trusting in him, after all we can do to evaluate a decision on our own, he will guide our feet. The path is his to reveal, but we have to step forward to make any progress."

He pauses briefly, drawing my attention again, and continues, "You may not know all you think you need to know right now, but you know enough to take the next step into the dark. You see, the people that achieve the most, the people who leave the biggest legacy and help the most people are simply the people who are quickest at taking those faith-guided steps into the dark. When faced with uncertainty, so many people freeze. They want to know. They want an assurance or a certainty about that next step. For some, this thinking simply slows their progress, for others it stops them dead in their tracks. For you, having the courage to take that next step quickly and with faith and courage is the key to everything you are hoping to achieve in life. By taking steps forward with faith quickly, you will achieve more, faster than you could have ever dreamed."

"But what if the steps I take are the wrong ones?" I interrupt.

"Please don't misunderstand. I'm not talking about running in the dark with reckless abandon. Rather, I'm talking about avoiding the excuse of over analyzing a situation or the excuse of waiting on assurance. I call these excuses because neither of them is real. Knowledge gained through analysis and assurance based on facts are only illusions before you take that step into the unknown. It is through taking action that you gain

both knowledge and assurance. Life and experience are not things that can be discovered through theory. You can only learn about them through action."

I nod in agreement. "That makes sense," I say. "But how do I know which direction I need to walk into the dark?", I ask.

"To answer that it is best to remember what the Savior invited us to do. He asked us to come follow him. When you don't know where you need to go, ask God what it is you need to do to follow the Savior now and what you can do to help others follow him, too. If you are always seeking to follow the Savior's example and to serve and lift others so they can come closer to him, then you can always take that step into the dark trusting that the Lord is guiding your path. Everything else are details that will come into focus as you move forward."

I nod in agreement again. I can feel in my heart that what he is telling me is true.

He continues, "The secret to the greatness you seek in life is found in moving forward with courage. When you courageously seek to serve others and to encourage and lift everyone you meet, you will find that the Lord has great things in store for you. The Lord has marvelous experiences prepared for you that you will receive as you act in faith. And you will find that as you move ahead into the dark your path will become clearer with each step. You will gain the assurances and knowledge you desire as you act. And step by step your ability to help others will grow exponentially."

"Stay the course and move ahead. You will do great things. You will touch the hearts of thousands helping them to understand truth. You will bless others and build a vast legacy of faith and love."

"What do I do, though, when I feel I am not enough?", I ask.

"Remember, everyone has times when they feel they are not enough. Whenever you are learning and growing, you will feel you are not enough, and that is exactly where you want to be. There, at the edges of your comfort zone, is where you will always find the greatest opportunity for growth and learning. Learn to value discomfort. Trust that when you feel you are not enough that you are the path to growth. As you do this your skills and abilities grow until eventually you will look back and see dramatic changes that you never realized were taking place. You will have moments when you look in the mirror and realize that the man looking back at you is not the man you remember being but is a better man you have become. That is how it works. Change happens gradually, but often we come to acknowledge it in *bursts of insight. Pay attention to the details of your daily life. This will ensure you become the man you want to be. You are always becoming someone, and it is always better to become someone you want to be. No one accidentally becomes the best version of themselves. That is only achieved with effort, focus and intentional action. So, continue to take deliberate steps forward and work to build the future you want. Focus on the truly important things in life with faith and know everything else are details that are easy to figure out when you get the big things right."*

As I sit listening, I can't help but remember the times when I had had such epiphanies. Times when I had seen one of my children sleeping and realized they were no longer toddlers. Times when I had looked in the mirror and seen that I had somehow become overweight. Times when the face I saw in the mirror was markedly older than I had been before. All times when the cumulative weight of so many small, almost imperceptible changes had suddenly become apparent. "I can see how that happens and how small changes can eventually add up to great things," I agree.

He nods and continues, "By small and simple things are great things brought to pass. All things follow this principle. As you give proper attention to the small but important things in life, you can make great progress. Be patient as your momentum builds and while you wait for the great changes to come." He pauses briefly and smiles again. "I am afraid the time has come for me to go."

"Already, you just got here?" I protest. "I still have so many questions…"

"I know, I know, and I wish I could stay longer and answer all of them, but unfortunately, that is not how this is supposed to work. Know this: the things I have already told you are what is truly important. The rest is just details." He chuckles again.

I chuckle too and look down at my hands. "Well…", I say, looking back up, but he is gone. "Well, if the rest is just details, then I guess I don't have anything to worry about," I say to myself. I close my eyes and smile. In a moment my wife and family join me.

"Sorry to keep you waiting," my wife says.

"No worry," I say. "I had a very insightful time waiting." I hold her hand and we smile at each other.

This was my experience of imagining what it would be like to meet my future self, a future version of me as I want to become. It contains a lot of information that is very useful to me, but which I hope may also help you. I have included this here with minimal edits from when I originally recorded for myself to give you an idea of how you can use your imagination to create your experience. What will your future self have to say to you?

Developing Your Vision

Faith knows it has received and acts accordingly.
— *Florence Shinn*

You can create your vision of what you want your future to be. This vision can bring power into your life as you make it as real as possible in your own mind. The more real you make the vision of your future, the more power-fully it can motivate you. It can direct your efforts as you strive to make your vision reality. The more real your vi-sion, the more motivation it can provide. Think about the details. Think of the specifics. What are the sights, sounds, smells and emotions that bring your vision to life? Think about them, hold them in your imagination, and write them down. Don't worry about whether you are writing poetic verse or the next best seller because you are only writing them down for yourself—but *write them down.*

Once you have taken the time to create your vision of the future and written it down, review it regularly so that it will remain fresh in your mind. Close your eyes and let yourself experience what it would feel like if your vi-sion for your future were *real.* This is a powerful way you can start to build hope and faith in your future. Let your mind and emotions experience what it will be like when your vision is reality. Then start acting in a way that fits with your vision. When you do this, your hope and faith will strengthen you and motivate you to keep striving for a future you truly want.

Foundation

Decide what you stand for. And then stand for it all the time.

— *Clayton M. Christensen*

Your vision of your future is a powerful tool. Your vision of where you want to go and who you want to become can transform your daily decisions and can give direction to everything you do. While it is important to have a powerful vision of who you want to become, just having a vision for your future is not enough on its own. Just like having a map doesn't get you to your destination, just having a vision won't make that vision a reality. Just like a map, your vision can help you know where you are going but in order to actually get there you need to take action. You need to put forth *effort*. You have to take action daily to build the future you desire.

Your journey to your vision, to the promised blessings the Lord has in store for you, is not a sprint. It isn't even a marathon. This journey is a lifelong process. To be successful in your journey, you will need a solid foundation of habits that will provide the basis for all your decisions and effort. As you establish this foundation, it will give you the ability to build your life and turn your vision into reality.

The Importance of a Strong Foundation

And now, my sons, remember, remember that it is upon the rock of our Redeemer, who is Christ, the Son of God, that ye must build your foundation; that when the devil shall send forth his mighty winds, yea, his shafts in the whirlwind, yea, when all his hail and his mighty storm shall beat upon you, it shall have no power over you to drag you down to the gulf of misery and endless wo, because of the rock upon which ye are built, which is a sure foundation, a foundation whereon if men build they cannot fall.

— Helaman 5:12

Whenever you are starting to build something, the first thing you must do is lay a foundation. This practice has been used for thousands of years. Many ancient buildings that still exist today are only here because their foundations were solid. In many other cases, archeologists have found ancient cities because the foundations of buildings still remain long after all other traces of the cities have vanished. Other ancient buildings, like the Leaning Tower of Pisa, serve as cautionary tales of what can happen when a building is built without an adequate foundation. The root of the word *foundation* is the Latin word *fundare*, which means *to lay a base for.* While we typically think of foundations as the base of a building, we also describe other things as *foundations.* In terms of ideas and principles, we describe principles as foundations. Also, we use the term foundation to describe organizations that are established with a sense of permanence. In each of these cases, foundations are a source of stability, permanence, and strength. Whether you are building a house, a skyscraper, a family or a life, if you want to succeed, you need to start by building a strong foundation.

It is easy for us to acknowledge the importance of a foundation when we think about a building. It is easy to see why a building cannot stand for long without a solid foundation to support its weight. When we think of more conceptual things like building a family or a life, the importance of a foundation is not immediately as clear. What does it mean to have a foundation for your life or a foundation for a family? How can you build such a foundation? What are the correct materials to use for such a foundation? How does it add strength and support everything else you do? If we want true stability in our lives, we must understand the answers to these questions. We must know how to build the right kind of foundation.

In one of his many parables, the Savior taught about the importance of having a solid personal foundation. In the parable of the wise and the foolish man, Jesus taught that the wise man builds his house on a foundation of rock. The foolish man, on the other hand, builds his house on a foundation of sand. In the parable, both men worked hard to build their houses. Eventually, a storm came that beat upon both of their houses. As the storm raged, the house that was built on the rock stood strong. Its solid foundation of rock gave it the strength it needed to weather the storms of life. The house built on the sandy foundation did not have this strength. As the storm raged, the sandy foundation washed away, causing that house to fall. As we read this parable, we learn that working to build a home is good, but despite our best efforts it will not be enough if the home is built on the wrong foundation. This leads us to ask what foundation we should use. How can we build on a foundation of rock?

In the parable, we are taught that the Savior and his gospel is the rock upon which we must build. The home we are building is a life of righteousness and discipleship. In such a life, Jesus Christ is the source of true power and stability. Striving to follow the commandments and going through the motions of being obedient is not enough. If those outward actions are not centered on Jesus Christ, then they simply aren't enough. When we build on the foundation of the Savior, we can have his power in our lives. One might ask, how is it possible to follow the commandments and not do so on a foundation of the Savior and his gospel? How can we build a testimony and *not* have it centered on Jesus Christ? Likewise, what can we do to ensure that we are building our lives with Jesus as the foundation for the things we do?

We can build our lives on the proper foundation as we make our faith in Jesus Christ and his Atonement the focus of our worship and obedience to the commandments. It is easy to go through the motions of living the gospel without having Christ be our focus. It is easy enough to attend church services and talk the talk of the gospel without actually letting the gospel sink deep into our hearts. Maybe you have experienced this yourself. Each of us has probably had times when we were outwardly participating in the gospel but were not feeling the peace and power it promises in our hearts. To gain the promised blessings of the gospel, we must open our hearts and strive to do our best, all the while relying on the Savior and his power to save. It is not enough to go through the motions of trying to become like Jesus, we must actually be *trying to become like Jesus*. We must be actively seeking to improve and sincerely working to repent when we sin. We must be striving to love and serve those around us as Jesus would if he were here. We must be doing our best to live the gospel both publicly and privately, trusting that the Lord is guiding our footsteps. That may sound like a lot to do and surely it is. In the next few sections, we will discuss how we can face this challenge without feeling completely overwhelmed.

Remember, we are on a long journey, we are not running a sprint or even a marathon. The Lord doesn't expect us to jump from the starting line to the finish line immediately. He does expect us to make progress, though, so let's talk about how we can do that.

What Is a Foundation?

> *Whether we are approaching behavior change as an individual, a parent, a coach, or a leader, we should ask ourselves the same question: "How can we design a world where it's easy to do what's right?" Redesigning your life so that actions that matter most are also the actions that are easiest to do.*
>
> — James Clear

When we talk about building a *foundation* in our personal lives, what are we talking about? Our foundations aren't made of rocks and concrete. Foundations in our personal lives are the habits we form that allow us to consistently act in some way. Whether our habits have been intentionally chosen or are habits that have just materialized over time, we are all creatures of habit. Our habits dictate our default behavior. They are the actions we do when we are not consciously doing something else. The best way to follow your vision and become the person you want to be in the future is to build a foundation of habits that are consistent with the future you want to create. When you create habits that help you act like the future you, you will rapidly become that person.

The challenge is to *intentionally* choose the habits you want to build then *practice* them until they become your default. When you choose your habits and practice until you have mastered them, you become the master of your fate. You can create whatever life you want. You can have hope that you can obtain the promises of the Lord in your life.

Start with Your Vision

We can't be true to ourselves if we don't know what we want, and more importantly why, so that's where we must begin.
— *Ryder Carroll*

The best way to predict your future is to create it.
— *Abraham Lincoln*

Like any long journey, the first step in building our foundation is knowing what we want to build. Your vision of your future can provide you with the blueprint and the raw material needed to begin building your foundation. Each of us can use our vision as a powerful tool for directing our actions and our plans for the future. Having a clear vision of where you want to go in life will give context to every decision you make. It can be the compass that directs the many decisions you make each daily. Because of this, it is critical for you to define and clarify your vision.

Gaining this clarity requires you to ponder and pray. You need to consider your desired future and what you need to do to get there. Honestly evaluate where you currently are in your journey. You then need to imagine your future and what it will be like when you get there. As you engage your imagination in this way, you will begin to see the changes you need to make in your life to get where you want to go. You will learn where you need to grow. You can identify the goals you need to pursue to progress towards the future you desire.

You can use many tools to help you as you ponder and pray about how to become your best self. One of the most powerful tools is writing in a journal. Writing your thoughts and aspirations in a journal can help you to process and clarify your thoughts. This writing does not need to be clean or follow a specific pattern. It does not need to be eloquent. It is not intended to be a record of your activities. Writing to organize your thoughts is very personal and is something you are writing strictly for yourself. Write in your journal to get your thoughts out of your head. Write your plans. Write your struggles. Write your successes.

As you write in your journal to process your thoughts, you will often discover important insights and truths that will help you in your efforts to improve. You will find that your plans become clearer and your progress towards your goals will be dramatically accelerated. In the next few sections, we will discuss some specific things you can write in your journal about that will help you gain more clarity and turn your journal into a powerful tool.

Gaining Clarity

The type of person you want to become—what the purpose of your life is—is too important to leave to chance. It needs to be deliberately conceived, chosen, and managed. The opportunities and challenges in your life that allow you to become that person will, by their very nature, be emergent.
— Clayton M. Christensen

Many people don't really know what they want their future to be. You might not have a clear vision of who you want to become in the future and what the Lord has in store for you. For many people, this is not something that they regularly think about. Most of us are so busy just trying to manage the challenges of our daily lives that we don't actively find time to think about who we want to become in the future. We don't take the time we need to understand what the Lord has planned for us and who he wants us to become. Each of us can learn more about what the Lord wants for our future. We can better understand what he wants us to achieve with the potential he has given us. But we need to put in the required effort to gain this understanding.

If you want a better understanding of what the Lord has in store for your life, you can start by trusting that the Lord will help you to gain a vision of what your future can become. If you haven't thought about it in a while, prayerfully ask the following questions to help you clarify what you want:

What do I love about my life right now?

What do I wish were different in my current life?

What have I always felt I want to do, but have not done yet?

How can I better serve those around me?

What type of person do I want to be in 3 years? How about in 5 years? How about in 10 years?

What aspect of the gospel do I find most challenging?

What can I do today to take one step closer to being the version of myself that I want to be?

What legacy do I want to leave?

What is the biggest thing I could do today to increase my faith?

One of the most important questions you can ask yourself are the following questions suggested by Brian Johnson:

1. *What's the #1 thing I could start doing today that, if I did it consistently, would have the most positive impact on my life? — then do it.*

2. *What's the #1 thing I could stop doing right now that, if I stopped doing it, would have the greatest positive impact on my life? — then quit doing it.*

— Brian Johnson

As you ask yourself these questions, write down your answers. Review the things you write and find what resonates with you. Take the time you need to ponder and seek guidance from the Holy Ghost. As you begin this process, don't worry at first about making sense of everything, just write it down. Get your ideas and hopes and dreams and concerns out of your head and into your journal. As you write these things down, you will gain insights into both what you may need to change in your life immediately and what you truly want your life to become. Let the impressions and insights you gain guide you as you start your journey. Regularly repeat this process any time you feel you need more direction.

You will find as you do this exercise that ideas will come that will inspire you to be a better person. You will gain a clearer vision of the person you want to become. Use this clarity to make a plan for the next steps in your journey. Write down what you need to do now to start becoming the person you want to be three, five, or thirty years in the future. Remember to record specific details so you can make your mental image of your hoped-for destination as real as possible. Having this clear vision and writing your next steps will help you build motivation and excitement. It will become the driving force behind your efforts to improve.

Creating Your Blueprint

> *If you should visit a ship in port and ask the captain for his port-of-call, he'll tell you in a single sentence. Even though the captain cannot see his port, his destination, for full 99% of the voyage, he knows it's there, and barring an unforeseen and highly unlikely catastrophe, he'll reach it. All he has to do is keep doing certain things every day.*
>
> *If someone asked you for your next port-of-call, your goal, could you tell him? Is your goal clear and concise in your mind? Do you have it written down? It's a good idea. We need reminding, reinforcement.*
>
> *— Earl Nightingale*

This quote talks about knowing where you are going. It is important that we determine what we want out of life. Despite what movies try to teach us, life will rarely just deliver your dreams on your doorstep. Discovering your dreams and vision rarely just *happens*. It takes effort and work. While you need to start with a vision, you will eventually need a plan if you are going to make significant progress towards your hopes and dreams.

Writing down your personal vision is the first step you need to take when figuring out who you want to become in this life. But it is only the first step. When Nephi was commanded to build a ship to cross the ocean to the promised land, he had absolute faith and hope that the Lord could get him and his family there. He knew where he wanted to go. Yet, he still had to determine what he needed to do to get there. Wanting to go to the promised land was not enough. Faith in the Lord was not enough. He had to find ore *and* make tools *and* chop down trees *and* mill them into lumber *and* build a ship *and* gather supplies *and* sail the ship across the ocean. All of these actions took thought and prayer and effort to execute.

If we are to find what we truly want in life and design a plan that will help us get there, we will have to search and do some mental digging. Writing in a journal is one of the best ways to do this searching. We have all heard about the importance of keeping a journal or a diary and of recording our personal history. While that kind of journal writing is important, it is not the type of journal writing we are talking about. Writing your thoughts and feelings in a journal is a powerful practice we can use to sort through our thoughts and feelings. Using a journal in this way will allow you to gain clarity about what we want in life. Your journal should be used to have a conversation with yourself. Record your thoughts and hopes for the future. Take time to think about the future you believe the Lord has in store for you and use your journal to organize your thoughts and feelings about that future. Write to talk to yourself about what you truly want. Don't worry what others may think about what you are writing.

This method of journal writing is not intended to record your past, it is a tool to help you create your future.

As you consistently use your journal in this way, you will gain a greater understanding of yourself. Journal writing will help you know what you want in your life. It will also increase your ability to identify impressions and guidance you receive from the Spirit along the way. You will start to know what is truly important to you. You will discover how you want to build your life.

If you feel overwhelmed with how to start writing in this way, you can learn from the many resources and journal writing practices out there. They can help you build momentum. Some of these include bullet journals, gratitude journals, morning pages, and many others. Which journal writing practice you choose is not as important as finding one that works for you and consistently using it to have that conversation with yourself. The more you continue to write in your journal the more powerful of a tool for change it will become.

Progress Takes Effort

Everything to do with becoming more like the Savior is difficult. For example, when God wanted to give the Ten Commandments to Moses, where did he tell Moses to go? Up on top of a mountain, on the top of Mount Sinai. So Moses had to walk all the way up to the top of that mountain to get the Ten Commandments. Now, Heavenly Father could have said, "Moses, you start there, and I'll start here, and I'll meet you halfway." Know, the Lord loves effort, because effort brings rewards that can't come without it.

— Russell M. Nelson

As you work to ponder, pray and journal about the person you want to become, remember that the actions you will take all require effort. It may be hard to clarify your vision of who you want to be. Use the commandments as a guide. The truths of the gospel will help us know what improvements we need to make. As you continue to learn where you need to improve, continue to invest your efforts in striving to follow the commandments at a higher level. The commandment to be perfect is meant to challenge us. It is meant to change us. We should expect that we will have to work to gain the blessings that are promised as we become more like our Savior.

The scriptures are full of stories of people who had to *do* something to progress in the path the Lord put before them. Moses and the Israelites had to walk across the dry ground of the parted Red Sea. Then they had to wander in the wilderness for 40 years. Those who followed the brother of Jared also trekked through the wilderness for years, building barges and crossing oceans. Likewise, Lehi's family spent years in the wilderness enduring hardships and toiling before they arrived at the promised land. Even in modern times, the pioneer saints were continually working to build the kingdom of God.

They erected temples, built beautiful cities where there had previously only been swamps, crossed a continent, and settled the American west. Each of these challenges required vast amounts of effort to overcome, but they transformed those stalwart men and women into people of profound faith and spiritual power.

You too can build similar faith and spiritual power as you work to become the person your Heavenly Father wants you to become. He will help you and guide you along the way, but you have to put in the work. However, as you strive to be better, you can trust that the Lord will magnify your effort to produce miracles in your life.

Building Your Gospel Foundation

The commandments are the foundation on which discipleship is built. Steady discipleship leads us to become firm, steadfast, and immovable, like the steel framework for a temple. This steady framework allows the Lord to send His Spirit to change our hearts. Experiencing a mighty change of heart is like adding beautiful features to the interior of a temple.

As we continue in faith, the Lord gradually changes us. We receive his image in our countenance and begin to reflect the love and beauty of his character. As we become more like him, we will feel at home in his house, and he will feel at home in ours.

— L. Whitney Clayton

No one "builds a house". They lay one brick again and again and again and the end result is a house. Nearly every big undertaking can be boiled down to a core unit of progress—its brick. A 45-minute gym visit is the brick of getting in great shape. A 30-minute practice session is the brick of becoming a great guitarist.

— Tim Urban

If the Gospel of Jesus Christ is the sure foundation for our lives, then our efforts to keep the commandments are the bricks used to build that foundation. As we strive each day to live the commandments, we steadily build that foundation one brick at a time. This daily effort to live the commandments will help us develop the habits of faith and righteousness. When we continue to build this foundation each day, it allows the Lord to purify our hearts. It helps us learn to love the Savior and each other more deeply.

Just as a house is built brick by brick, you build your future day by day. If you look closely, you can probably see this truth in action in your life right now. You are an expert at living the life you are currently living. Your life as it currently exists has been built by your habits and routines. These habits are something you very likely don't have to think about much anymore. You probably don't even have to try very hard to be the person you are now. Each of the habits and routines that make up your days are the bricks you are actively using to build your current life.

The key to building a great future is to build great days. Each day we need to ask ourselves what we can do today to take a step closer to becoming the person we want to be in the future. What big or little thing can we do that will not only bring us closer to our desired future, but will make that future inevitable? As we take the time to choose the things we do each day, we can build with the best bricks. We can build the life we truly desire. The best way to become the person you want to be in the future is to start *today* to act as that person would act. Do the things that the best version of you would do. The sooner you start to behave in a way that is consistent with who you want to become, the sooner you will become that person. These actions do not happen on their own, especially when we are trying to change the course of our lives. This takes consistent work and effort.

Don't let the challenge of applying this effort overwhelm and frustrate you, though. Yes, building new habits can be challenging, but it is also something you can do a little bit at a time. We are not commanded to run faster than we have strength, but we are commanded to be diligent. Just like a builder placing bricks one at a time to build a house, you can take small actions one at a time to build new habits. These actions may feel small, but as we are taught in the Book of Mormon, "By small and simple things are great things brought to pass" (Alma 37:6). When we approach the challenge of building ourselves into the people we want to become, we can prevent feeling overwhelmed when we remember that we can achieve great things as we focus on the right small things. You can do this. You can succeed.

Check Your Progress Often

From the Lord's perspective, establishing the finest homes has everything to do with the personal qualities of the people who live there. These homes aren't made fine in any important or lasting way by their furniture or by the net worth or social status of the people who own them. The finest characteristic of any home is the image of Christ reflected in the home's residents. What matters is the interior design of the souls of the inhabitants, not the structure itself.

— L. Whitney Clayton

Remember that the foundation we are building is not something separate from the rest of our lives. Rather, it is the basis for everything we do. Because of this, we can strengthen our foundation in everything we do.

We can strengthen our spiritual foundation when we are kind to others. We can strengthen our foundation when we take time and really listen to our family and friends. We can strengthen our foundation when we serve those around us. We can strengthen our foundation as we seek to follow the guidance of the Holy Ghost. We can strengthen our foundation when we feel gratitude for the many blessings we have. In short, we can strengthen our spiritual foundation as we strive to follow the commandments in every aspect of our lives. This does not require us to carve out large amounts of time in our schedule to study the scriptures or to spend hours a day praying. It does require that we actively strive to live the gospel in everything we do.

This can be difficult. As we do our best to live the gospel throughout the day, we must remember that progress is more important than perfection. That is worth repeating, *progress is more important than perfection.*

The voyage of the best ship is a zigzag line of a hundred tacks. See the line from a sufficient distance, and it straightens itself to the average tendency.

— Ralph Waldo Emerson

Change is hard. No really, change is HARD. As such, expect that you will have challenges as you work to improve and build a wonderful future. You are changing yourself into a new person. You are becoming the person who lives at a higher level. But you aren't that person yet. You will encounter obstacles as you work to build new habits and become a new person. When you encounter trials and setbacks, remember to look at your successes and try not to dwell on your perceived failures.

You are trying to become a powerful spiritual follower of Jesus Christ. As you work towards that goal, there will be times that you stumble. But there will also be times when you succeed. While it is important to repent and recommit ourselves when we sin, we also need to be merciful with ourselves. We need to recognize the growth and successes we experience as we strive to follow the Savior.

> *Measure the GAIN, not the GAP.*
>
> — *Dan Sullivan*

Remember that as you work each day to be better you are steering the course of your life. Look at the overall change in who you are becoming. Take time to acknowledge the improvements you have made. When you acknowledge the improvements you make, you can guard yourself from the frustration of the minor upsets you will surely encounter along the way. When we measure our current progress against the ideal of perfection, we are measuring the *gap*. When we measure our progress in this way, you will always find yourself falling short of the ideal. This can lead to guilt, disappointment and frustration. When you measure your progress against how you used to be, you are measuring the *gain*. Measuring the gain allows you to see how much growth you have experienced. When you measure the gains you have seen, you can experience the happiness and confidence that comes as you continually improve. As you consistently strive to be the person you want to become, you can see improvement each day. Eventually you will become the person you long to be.

The Lord knows we are not perfect. He loves to bless us when we show our desires to follow him. He will bless us each and every time we make an effort to draw nearer to him. As we strive to do this each day, we will inevitably draw closer to him. We will consistently become more like him. Daily effort to draw closer to the Savior is the foundation we need to build. It is our daily efforts that become the foundation that allows us to endure and grow from the trials and challenges we encounter in life.

How Can We Make Course Corrections?

Every one of us, if we would reach perfection, must at one time ask ourselves this question, "What lack I yet?"

— *Harold B. Lee*

During our journey to become like our Savior we will all have times when we will fall short. Despite our best intentions to live the commandments, we will have times when we don't. What should we do when this happens?

In the Bible, we are told the story of a young man who was living an exemplary life. He was doing everything he had been taught to do. He came to Jesus Christ to ask the question, "What lack I yet?" and was told what he needed to do to improve. Regardless of what your goals you have for the future, it is important that we regularly ask the Lord what we need to do to improve. Ask your Heavenly Father in prayer, "What lack I yet?" If you ask this question sincerely and listen for an answer, you will receive impressions from the Holy Ghost. He will tell you what you need to do to increase the blessings of the gospel in your life. The impressions you feel may surprise you. You may feel prompted to clean up your language. You may feel prompted to clean up your room. You may feel prompted to stop being negative. You may be told to be more diligent in your prayers or scripture study. You may feel impressed to do one of these or any of a million other things. You will be told what you can do to gain the Spirit in your life more fully. You will receive guidance that will allow you to draw closer to Jesus Christ.

I have asked this question many times in my life. Without fail I have always felt impressions that, when followed, have helped me draw closer to my Savior. I know that if you sincerely ask for his help and do your best to follow the impressions you receive you will also be blessed. As you work to build your spiritual foundation, your vision of that future will clarify. Take the time to review your progress and evaluate what you need to do next. Taking the time to ask, "What lack I yet?" will help you to determine the areas where you need to improve and will lead to an increase of the Spirit of the Lord in your life.

Standing in Holy Places

> *Our ultimate quest in life is to prepare to meet our Maker. We do this by striving daily to become more like our Savior, Jesus Christ. And we do that as we repent daily and receive his cleansing, healing, and strengthening power. Then we can feel enduring peace and joy, even during turbulent times. This is exactly why the Lord has implored us to stand in holy places and "be not moved."*
> — *Russell M. Nelson*

The work of improving our lives and becoming more like our Heavenly Father and our Savior is an effort that will last our entire lives. As we continue in that effort, we will learn and grow. Sometimes we will also stumble and fall. When we encounter challenges and are brought face to face with our weaknesses, we must take time to repent and holy places. As we strive to follow the gospel more perfectly in our daily lives, we will have times that we fall short of being like Jesus Christ. Our Heavenly Father knows we are not perfect and has provided us a way to overcome our imperfection. Repentance allows us and to overcome our weaknesses through Jesus Christ. Repentance gives us the hope we need to stand up and try again to follow the Savior's example each time we stumble and fall. Regardless of whether we have always suc-ceeded in following him in the past, we can repent and try again today.

We can gain strength to do this as we stand in holy places. When we hear the term "holy places" we often think of the temple. The temples of the Lord truly are holy places, but we can also work to make many other holy places where we can draw closer to our Heavenly Father. Our churches, our homes, out in nature, and many other places can become holy places for us if we let them. We can make these places holy as we do what we can to make them places where we can increasingly feel the Spirit of the Lord.

What are your holy places?
Where do you go to gain spiritual strength?
How often do you intentionally stand in holy places?
What can you change in your life to allow you to stand in holy places more often?

As with all important things, building a sure spiritual foundation takes time and effort. We must work to build a spiritual foundation for our lives. Remember, the Lord is waiting to bless us as soon as we start putting forth sin-cere effort. He will guide us and help us as we strive to follow him. With his help, we can do everything we need to do. With his help, we can build a foundation for our lives that can give us strength and security amid all our trials and tribulations. It is my hope and prayer that each of us can continually find ways to make our spiritual foundations stronger. By so doing, we can draw closer to our Savior, Jesus Christ. We can become a little bit more like him each day.

Practice

For behold, thus saith the Lord God: I will give unto the children of men line upon line, precept upon precept, here a little and there a little; and blessed are those who hearken unto my precepts, and lend an ear unto my counsel, for they shall learn wisdom; for unto him that receiveth I will give more; and from them that shall say, We have enough, from them shall be taken away even that which they have.

— *2 Nephi 28:30*

In the previous chapter, we talked about building our foundation on the gospel of Jesus Christ. In gospel terms, this foundation is your testimony of the Atonement of Jesus Christ and the truth of the teachings of the gospel. This foundation is extremely important. But a foundation is not a house. A firm testimony is only the start of our journey to become more like our Savior.

Once we have started to have a foundation, the next step is to begin building upon that foundation. We must do the work to build the house. We must do the work to build our testimony. As we are taught in the quote above from 2 Nephi, the Lord gives us knowledge line upon line, precept upon precept. This is how our testimonies grow. Earlier in this book we talked about how no one *builds a house*, but rather they add one brick at a time until eventually they have built a house. This can lead us to ask the question: when does that pile of bricks turn into a house? When do our small and simple acts of faith turn into a testimony? When do our consistent acts of service and obedience become a righteous life?

The Sorites Paradox

It can often feel like having a righteous life or a strong testimony is a destination that we will arrive at some time in the future. We might feel we have to press forward on our journey, enduring mediocrity until some future day when we *arrive* and finish our journey. If you have viewed your gospel journey in this way, you know that this can feel extremely frustrating. It can be easy, when you have this perspective, to feel like your efforts to live the gospel won't be rewarded. You may even feel you are being asked to pay an overwhelming debt when you only can make the occasional small payment. When we start to feel this way, we can greatly increase our hope by changing our perspective. We can learn to have hope during our gospel journey. We can learn to show gratitude for our blessings each day.

In the 4th century BCE, the Greek philosopher Eubulides of Miletus was known for his use of paradoxes as a method for understanding truth. One of his thought experiments is called the Sorites Paradox or The Paradox of the Heap (*Sorites* is derived from the Greek word for *heap*). This paradox may help us better understand the value of the small daily steps we take on our journey of faith. The Paradox of the Heap goes something like this:

A single grain of sand is certainly not a heap. Nor is the addition of a single grain of sand enough to transform a non-heap into a heap: when we have a collection of grains of sand that is not a heap, then adding but one single grain will not create a heap. And yet we know that at some point we will have a heap.

— *Wikipedia*

The premise of the paradox is that we would not call a single grain of sand a *heap of sand*. But, as we add grains of sand, one at a time, eventually, the pile of sand becomes what we would call a *heap of sand*. The addition of the seemingly trivial grains of sand, eventually gives us the heap of sand. But which grain of sand changed it into a heap? If, at one point, the pile of sand is *not* a heap and when we add just one more grain of sand it *becomes* a heap then that means that each and every grain of sand is important. Because there isn't a definitive way to know which grain of sand turns the pile of sand into a heap each grain of sand counts.

You can view this paradox in the opposite direction as well. Suppose you had a heap of sand that contained 1,000,000 grains of sand. If you remove *just one* grain of sand, you now have a heap of sand that contains 999,999 grains of sand. Arguably, this is still a *heap*. But what if you repeatedly remove grains of sand? Eventually, you will have only one grain of sand left. Is that single grain of sand still a *heap*? The Paradox of the Heap claims that because removing a single grain of sand would turn a *heap of sand* into something that is not a *heap of sand*, then even a single grain of sand is a *heap.*

Why is this important? Why am I risking boring you with the details of an Ancient Greek thought experiment? Because our actions in life are just like the grains of sand in the paradox. Our daily acts of faith and obedience are our grains of sand and the pile of sand we are creating is our personal heap of righteousness. Each and every day we are faced with countless decisions and opportunities where we must choose how we will act. Will we follow the Savior's example, or will we succumb to our natural tendencies? Will we put others' needs before our own or follow our selfish impulses? These decisions may seem inconsequential when viewed individually. And like single grains of sand, they might be. But when viewed as a whole, they add up. They are not inconsequential. They are our personal heap of righteousness. They are the building blocks of our habits. Though they are small, they will become our character.

To look at it another way, a single kind word may not be what makes us more Christlike, but a habit of kindness will. Reading a single verse of scripture will not help us understand the Gospel deeply, but a habit of regularly studying the scriptures will. Repenting of a single sin will not make us holy. But repenting daily will lead us back to our heavenly home. Because of this, each act of kindness, each session of scripture study, and each attempt to repent becomes profoundly important. They are the bricks we are using to build our spiritual homes.

They are the grains of sand that will eventually allow us to become righteous disciples of the Savior, Jesus Christ.

In this section of this book, we will talk about principles that can help each of us to pick the right bricks to use as we build our spiritual homes. What are the most important practices and habits to cultivate? How can we consistently take the actions that make us more like Jesus Christ? As we take time to identify the most important actions that we need to take then regularly do those actions, we can each see a dramatic change in our lives. We will see an increase of the Spirit. We will see an increase in our righteousness. We will see our own grains of sand become a heap.

The 80/20 Rule, the Gospel, and You

Of course it's hard. Everything to do with becoming more like the Savior is difficult. The Lord loves effort, because effort brings rewards that can't come without it.

— Russell M. Nelson

Let us put our faith in the Lord Jesus Christ into action!

— Russell M. Nelson

80% of the results come from 20% of the causes. A few things are important; most are not.

— Richard Koch

In order to use the best bricks as we build our lives and our testimonies, we must learn how to seek and receive personal revelation. We all have unique challenges, struggles, and stewardship and we all experience different circumstances. If we are to discover what the Lord wants us to do, we need to know how to hear him. We each have a limited amount of time and energy. Because of this it is critical to know what activities are most important for us to focus on. As we increase our ability to receive personal revelation, the Lord will guide us in our efforts. When we know how to feel and follow the impressions of the Holy Ghost, we can tap into the direction the Lord is waiting to give us. In the scriptures we are told that the Holy Ghost will teach us all things that we need to do. To benefit from this great blessing, we must know how to listen to the Spirit.

As we think about which activities in our lives deserve our attention, it can be helpful to consider the 80/20 rule. The 80/20 rule can help us in our efforts to live the gospel.

The 80/20 rule, also known as the Perato Principle, states that 80% of results come from 20% of our efforts. Conversely, the remaining 20% of results come from the remaining 80% of our efforts. Research has shown that typically 20% of the activities that lead to 80% of the results. This principle has proven to be a reality in the world in nearly every area of life. It is also true in your life.

What does it mean when we say 80% of results come from 20% of our efforts? It means that not all activities have equal value. Not every important thing is equally important. In pretty much *every* endeavor, some activities are more valuable than others. In most endeavors, a critical few activities are *significantly* more valuable than other activities. This holds true whether you are looking at business, personal growth, or gospel living. In each of these disciplines—and practically every other aspect of life—we find far more activities vying for our time and attention than we have time to complete. You must choose which of the many available tasks and activities you will spend your time and effort on. Many of the activities you can choose are helpful and good. But only a few of these activities are critical in gaining true success.

Since we do not have the time and energy to do everything, it is important to determine the few *critical* things that have the greatest value. By finding the most important things we can focus our time and energy on activities that will have the yield the greatest results. As we work to live the gospel, we can use the 80/20 rule to focus our efforts on the truly essential activities that will bring the greatest blessings and growth in our lives.

Big Rocks

Putting first things first means organizing and executing around your most important priorities. It is living and being driven by the principles you value most, not by the agendas and forces surrounding you.

— *Stephen R. Covey*

As you begin to identify the most important activities you need to focus on in your life, you need to organize your life to allow you to give those activities the time and attention they deserve. Life can be messy and busy. Because of this, knowing that an activity is important is often not enough to make it part of our daily routine. For example, everyone knows they should eat healthy food and exercise regularly, but many of us who struggle to do so. Now that you are starting to identify the most important 20% of activities in your life, how do you make sure you are doing them? The most effective way I have found to understand this is an object lesson popularized by Stephen R. Covey. This object lesson is called "Big Rocks." It goes something like this:

We each have one life and we each have a finite amount of time. We can represent our life and time as a large glass jar.

We can choose how we will fill our jar of life. We all have before us a vast selection of activities we can choose to place in our jar. At some point our jar will be full. When the jar is full, we are out of time and can no longer add activities to our life. We will represent these activities as rocks of various sizes. Some of these rocks are large and some of them are small. Some of them are so small that they may just be a grain of sand. The size of these rocks indicates how *important* they are and how much *time* they require.

The big rocks are very important. They represent the activities that will have the most profound effect on building the future you dream of. Sometimes they may also take a lot of your time. The big rocks are the important 20% of your activities that yield 80% of the results in your life.

The smaller rocks are not as important or time consuming as the big rocks. They often represent the daily necessities of living life. These include things like making your bed, doing the dishes, or paying your bills. They are important in the context of living each day, but don't directly help you reach your future dreams.

The smallest rocks and grains of sand are unimportant things of life. They are the distractions and time wasters we all indulge in from time to time. They may sometimes seem urgent but in reality they are unimportant.

As the owner of your life, it is your responsibility to determine how and when you add the various rocks to your jar. For many people, this is not an intentional choice they make, but rather the result of life just "happening." When we take this approach, we start by adding a lot of sand and small rocks to our jar first. We get caught up in just getting by. We do the tasks that are screaming for our attention. We distract ourselves with mindless tasks like scrolling on social media to help manage the stress we feel. Eventually, as a final effort we may try to fit in the big rocks.

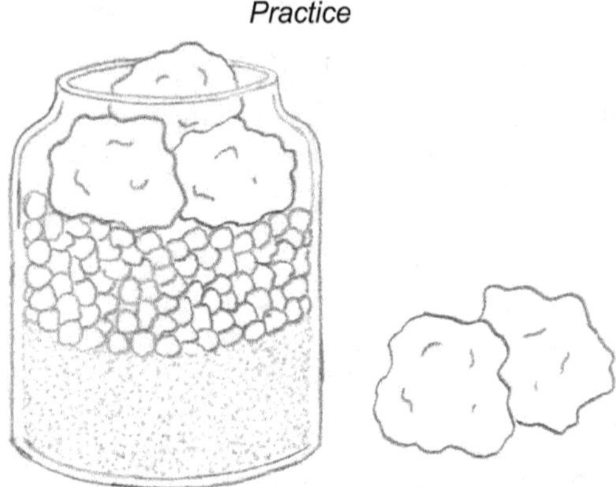

The problem is that when we go to add the big rocks, we find we can no longer fit them all in the jar. We end up feeling unfulfilled and guilty, knowing we didn't complete our most important tasks. We simply run out of time.

When you take a more intentional approach to what you add to our life, you start by adding the biggest rocks first. Only when you finish adding the big rocks do you then start to add the smaller rocks. Finally, you add the sand. The result of this is that *everything* fits in the jar.

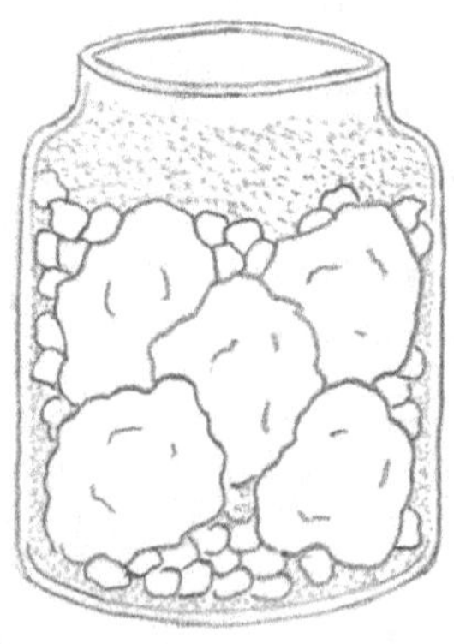

Taking such an intentional approach to how we spend our time and energy allows us to achieve the most important things in life. It also allows us to do many—if not all—of the other things we desire to do. The best thing about this approach is that it allows us to take care of the most important things in life. When we have taken care of the most important things, we can enjoy the many other activities we need to do without the guilt or stress.

As you approach each day, think about how you are adding rocks to your personal jar. Are you taking care of the most important things first, or are you getting distracted by the many trivial things in life? If you aren't sure how you are doing, you can consider how you feel at the end of each day. When you lay down to sleep at night, do you feel frustrated and guilty, or do you feel content and fulfilled? For most of us, we are somewhere between these two extremes. If we want to do the most important things, we need to identify the big rocks in our lives and make sure we give them the attention they deserve before we spend time and energy on other things. If we don't put in the effort to determine our priorities, we run the risk of spending all our time on the 80% of activities that only give us 20% of the results we desire. When we do this, we fail to give time to the 20% of activities that would yield the greatest 80% of results.

What Is Your 20 Percent?

When we seek to hear—truly hear—His Son, we will be guided to know what to do in any circumstance.

As we seek to be disciples of Jesus Christ, our efforts to hear him need to be ever more intentional. It takes conscious and consistent effort to fill our daily lives with His words, His teachings, His truths.

— Russell M. Nelson

We can seek the Lord's help in determining what 20% of practices and activities will lead to the greatest spiritual blessings in our lives. We are all at different places in our journey of life. Because of this, we will each have different areas where we need to focus *now*. As we seek to grow spiritually, we can pray and ask for our Heavenly Father for guidance. Through the Spirit, the scriptures, and the words of modern prophets our Heavenly Father will help us know what things deserve our greatest attention.

Over the years, Church leaders have repeatedly counseled us to seek the guidance of the Spirit to identify the most important activities in our lives. They have also counseled us to be intentional about giving our time and effort to these most important efforts. In the next few chapters, we will discuss some of those teachings.

Good, Better, Best

> *We should begin by recognizing the reality that just because something is good is not a sufficient reason for doing it. The number of good things we can do far exceeds the time available to accomplish them. Some things are better than good, and these are the things that should command priority attention in our lives.*
>
> *— Dallin H. Oaks*

We all have a variety of activities available to us each day. One of the biggest challenges we face is to choose between activities that have true value over other activities that are merely good. This exemplifies the 80/20 rule very well. Undoubtedly, some of the 80% of low value activities we can choose are not "bad" things. They just aren't the "best" things we could do. And, when we spend so much time on these lower value "good" things, we can often fail to give attention to the "best" things we have available to us. There is nothing wrong with hobbies or church planning meetings. But those activities, while serving some purpose, are not the best and most important activities. They are the small and medium rocks we add to our jar.

The most important activities are those that will truly bring the power of the gospel to life in our hearts, homes and the lives of others. These activities will reinforce our gospel foundations. They will build us into the people the Lord has created us to be. They will bring us closer to our Heavenly Father in significant ways.

> *The only things that really need to be accomplished in the home are daily scripture study and prayer and weekly family home evening.*
>
> *— Linda S. Reeves*

When it comes to living the gospel in our homes, very few activities are critical. Personal and family scripture study–especially study of Come Follow Me, personal and family prayer, and Family Home Evening are all critical in turning our homes and our lives into sanctuaries of faith.

Years ago, the leaders of the Church did a study of what practices lead the youth of the church to reaching major gospel milestones. These milestones included going to the temple for their personal endowment, marriage in the temple, and for young men receiving the Melchizedek Priesthood and serving an honorable mission. The study examined a host of influences and activities to try and determine which activities helped produce these gospel outcomes. When the results of the study came back, the *only* activities that showed significant correlation to the desired outcomes were personal and family scripture study and personal and family prayer. These activities had a correlation of over 90% to the gospel outcomes. This means that 90% of people who had regular personal and family scripture study and personal and family prayer eventually made it to the temple and started their own eternal families. This is worth saying again, *the only* practices that had any significant relation to gaining the long-term blessings of the temple and the priesthood were consistent personal and family scripture study and personal and family prayer. It is no wonder that we are so often counseled to make these practices part of our daily life. This does not mean that other activities are not also important. But it does mean that scripture study and prayer are vital to anyone who wants to gain the blessings of the gospel more fully in their life.

What Lack I Yet?

The journey of discipleship is not an easy one. It has been called a "course of steady improvement." As we travel along that straight and narrow path, the Spirit continually challenges us to be better and to climb higher. The Holy Ghost makes an ideal traveling companion. If we are humble and teachable, He will take us by the hand and lead us home.

— Larry R. Lawrence

When we seek to hear—truly hear—His Son, we will be guided to know what to do in any circumstance.

— *Russell M. Nelson*

We all have different challenges and trials. We also all have different shortcomings and weaknesses. One of the most beautiful truths of the gospel is that it can be immediately valuable to each of us regardless of where we are in our personal spiritual journey. No matter who you are or where you are spiritually right now, the Lord can help you know what steps you can take today to draw nearer to him.

I previously referenced the New Testament story of the young man who came to Jesus to ask the question, "What lack I, yet?" The Lord, after hearing of the many commandments the young man was diligently following, told the young man to sell all that he had and give to the poor and to come and follow him. In the story, the young man went away grieving because he was not ready to follow that instruction, but we can learn a lot from his example of asking the Lord, "What lack I, yet?"

When we humbly ask the Lord, "What lack I, yet?" and listen to the impressions of the Spirit, the Lord will instruct us. We will receive guidance for changes we can make that are right along the boundary between our righteous hearts and our natural tendencies. These impressions will stretch us and challenge us. This shouldn't be a surprise because it is in the stretching and challenging that we learn and grow. As we ask the Lord what we can do to improve and follow the guidance we receive, we can make continual progress on the path of righteousness. When we do our best to follow the guidance we receive, we can see massive spiritual power and growth in our lives. We don't need to worry about trying to do everything. We don't need to run faster than we have strength. But we do need to be diligent and do the most important things. Asking, "What lack I, yet?" will help us know what the most important things are for us in our daily efforts to follow the Savior.

Personal Worship

Loving God and loving our neighbors are the doctrinal foundation of ministering; home-centered, Church-supported learning; Sabbath-day spiritual worship; and the work of salvation on both sides of the veil. All of these things are based on the divine commandments to love God and to love our neighbors. Can there be anything more basic, fundamental, and simpler than that?

Living the true, pure, and simple gospel plan will allow us more time to visit the widows, widowers, orphans, lonely, sick, and poor. We will find peace, joy, and happiness in our life when serving the Lord and our neighbors.

The Sabbath-day adjustments that emphasize home-centered, Church-supported gospel learning and studying are an opportunity to renew our spirit and our devotion to God within the walls of our homes. What could possibly be more simple, basic, and profound? Brothers and sisters, can you see that learning and teaching the gospel in our families is an important way to find joy and happiness in our lives?

— M. Russell Ballard

Each of us can gain a greater measure of spiritual power in our lives as we engage in humble and intentional personal worship. Like the oil in the ten virgins' lamps, we cannot borrow our spiritual power from others, and we can only rely on light from other people's testimonies for so long. If we desire to experience the many blessings our Father in Heaven has prepared for us, we need to increase the quality of our personal worship. We need to live the gospel and allow it to sink deep into our hearts. As we do this, the Lord will transform us into the people he knows we can be.

Unlocking the Power of Personal Worship

Over the past several years a lot has changed in the church. Ministering has replaced home and visiting teaching. Come Follow Me has replaced a variety of lesson plans. The new Children and Youth program has replaced scouting and personal progress. A new focus on home-centered, church supported worship has replaced the previous Sunday meeting schedule with a new schedule that invites us to focus more on living the gospel in our homes as part of our daily lives.

As I have participated in these various changes, I have had the feeling that these changes were made to help us increase the quality of our personal worship. They invite each of us to live in a way that will bring the Spirit and blessings of the gospel into our lives more fully. This is because the power and promise of the gospel is the great change it can make in your life when you choose to live it. It has the power to help you be someone better than you now are. It has the power to help you become like Jesus Christ. But to access this power, you have to make the gospel an active force in your life. You need to engage in daily practices of personal worship.

I have a favorite story that comes to mind every time I think about personal worship.

A tourist visiting England's Eton College asked the gardener how he got the lawns so perfect. "That's easy," he replied, "You just brush off the dew every morning, mow them every other day, and roll them once a week."

"Is that all?" asked the tourist.

"Absolutely," replied the gardener. "Do that for 500 years and you'll have a nice lawn, too."

— The Pragmatic Programmer

What I love about this short story is the way it teaches the truth that by small and simple things, great things are brought to pass. More importantly, it is by *consistently* doing the small and simple things that great things are brought to pass in our lives. Just like a lawn or a garden, our testimonies need constant care and upkeep. Our personal holiness and conversion to the gospel are the natural result of our ongoing efforts to live the gospel each day. To gain these blessings we must be diligent in doing the things the Lord has commanded us to do. We must consistently pray, read the scriptures, and do other acts of personal worship.

Finding Power Through Personal Worship

How do you honor the Sabbath Day? In my much younger years, I studied the work of others who had compiled lists of things to do and things not to

> *do on the Sabbath. It wasn't until later that I learned from the scriptures that my conduct and my attitude on the Sabbath constituted a sign between me and my Heavenly Father. With that understanding, I no longer needed lists of dos and don'ts. When I had to make a decision whether or not an activity was appropriate for the Sabbath, I simply asked myself, "What sign do I want to give to God?" That question made my choices about the Sabbath Day crystal clear.*
>
> *— Russell M. Nelson*

Have you ever felt like you were doing all the things we are taught to do in the gospel, but not seeing the promised rewards? Perhaps you attend church, read your scriptures and pray, but don't feel you have the Spirit in your life as you would expect. Maybe you find that you feel burdened by responsibilities rather than blessed by the opportunities to serve. Or, maybe you have burning questions about the gospel and are seeking answers in prayer, but feel that the heavens are silent. It could be that you attend the temple, but don't leave there with the peace in your heart you had hoped to receive.

All of these actions are acts of personal worship. If you have wondered why your personal worship has not yielded the results you were hoping for, you are not alone. Many of us desire to have better, more impactful experiences with our personal worship. So how do we do that? How can we make personal worship a powerful tool for bringing the Spirit into our lives and drawing us closer to our Heavenly Father?

Sometimes we may be doing all we can to follow the gospel, but we may still need to wait on the Lord for answers. Throughout the scriptures and church history, we hear many stories of people who endured trials with faith as they waited on the Lord to send blessings, they so desperately desired. When we are doing our best to wait patiently on the Lord, we can remember the stories of Nephi being tied up on the ship during a terrible storm, Alma and Amulek being cast into prison, the Prophet Joseph Smith suffering for months in the Liberty jail, and countless experiences of the early Latter-day Saints and they were driven from their homes repeatedly. Sometimes we are asked to wait or endure trials because the Lord is preparing us for greater blessings. Sometimes we are given such challenges to try our faith. When we do our best to hold on to our faith and trust in the Lord, he can turn every trial into a blessing. He will strengthen us through our trials.

But what about the times when we are doing our best to live the commandments and are still struggling to feel the blessings of the gospel? How can we engage in more powerful personal worship? As Russell M. Nelson taught above, for many of us we often get caught in the trap of viewing the gospel and our worship as a list of dos and don'ts. If you have done this, you are not alone. Most of us have created a dos and don'ts list at some point in our gospel journey. While we usually take this approach to try and clarify what we need to do, it can often lead to stress, uncertainty, doubt and frustration. Additionally, approaching the gospel as a simple list of dos and don'ts can prevent the power and truth of the gospel from penetrating our hearts and changing us into more Christlike people.

Elder Nelson teaches us that a better way is to ask the question, "What sign do I want to give to God?" This question should be at the center of our personal worship. When we seek to show God, through our actions, that we love him and are seeking to follow him, we can unlock the power of the gospel in our lives. Regularly asking this question can improve the quality of our worship and bring the blessings of the gospel into your lives with greater power and strength. This does require effort. It requires us to do the spiritual work of striving to do all we can to draw closer to our Heavenly Father. But when we sincerely strive to draw near to him, we will be blessed.

> *My beloved brothers and sisters, I plead with you to increase your spiritual capacity to receive revelation. Choose to do the spiritual work required to enjoy the gift of the Holy Ghost and hear the voice of the Spirit more frequently and more clearly.*
>
> *— Russell M. Nelson*

I recently heard something that made me laugh, but which highlights a mental trap we all occasionally fall victim to. I was watching a talk show where they were taking questions from audience members. Someone wrote in a question that went something like this:

> *"I want to learn to be an expert piano player, what is the quickest way I can do that without having to practice?"*

When we hear that question, most of us immediately realize the absurdity of the question. The answer, of course, is that there is no way to become an expert piano player without practice. It is the same with building a testimony, gaining power in the priesthood, becoming more charitable, gaining more power through scripture study, or making the Sabbath a delight in our lives. Each of us build those attributes and gain the blessings promised for those acts of worship through practice. Daily. Consistent. Practice.

We must practice if we are to learn a skill like playing the piano and we must do the spiritual work to build our testimonies and spiritual power. There is no other way.

If you feel you are putting forth sincere effort to follow the commandments, but still are not feeling the power of the Spirit in your life, you can ask the Lord for guidance about what you need to do to improve. Ask him for help and insights. Listen to the feelings in your heart. Then do your best to follow the guidance you receive. As you strive to do this, you will continue to have an increase of spiritual power in your life.

The Power of Consistency

In the New Testament, the Savior teaches the parable of the ten virgins. You remember the story. It goes something like this:

The Bridegroom (Christ) announces that it is time for the wedding feast. It is dark outside, so the ten virgins need to use lamps to light their way at the wedding feast. Five of the virgins have oil for their lamps and five do not.

The five virgins who need oil try to borrow some from the other five, but the five with oil do not have enough to share with those who are unprepared. The prepared virgins go to the wedding. The unprepared virgins rush to find oil. They eventually find oil, but by the time they arrive to the wedding they are too late. The door was locked, and they were not permitted to enter.

Elder David A. Bednar taught us a little about this parable. He said:

Were the five wise virgins selfish and unwilling to share, or were they indicating correctly that the oil of conversion cannot be borrowed? Can the spiritual strength that results from consistent obedience to the commandments be given to another person? Can the knowledge obtained through diligent study and pondering of the scriptures be conveyed to one who is in need? Can the peace felt by someone faithfully living the gospel be transferred to an individual experiencing adversity or great challenge? The clear answer to each of these questions is no.

As the wise virgins emphasized properly, each of us must "buy for ourselves." These inspired women were not describing a business transaction; rather, they were emphasizing our individual responsibility to keep our lamp of testimony burning and to obtain an ample supply of the oil of conversion. This precious oil is acquired one drop at a time—"line upon line and precept upon precept" (2 Nephi 28:30), patiently and persistently. No shortcut is available; no last-minute flurry of preparation is possible.

— *David A. Bednar*

The way we keep our lamps filled with oil is by consistently doing the work of filling them. True power of testimony, power in the priesthood, and charity are all attributes that must be cultivated over time. They cannot be obtained through desperate last-minute effort. Rather, the spiritual oil of testimony and gospel power is collected one drop at a time with each and every gospel-related action we take. Just as we discussed with building a foundation or a house one brick at a time or adding grains of sand one at a time until you have a giant heap of sand, so too, we must gather our spiritual strength bit by bit until it becomes a powerful force in our life that can light our way back to the Savior.

Seeking God's Power

Wherefore, my beloved brethren, pray unto the Father with all the energy of heart, that ye may be filled with this love, which he hath bestowed upon all who are true followers of his Son, Jesus Christ; that ye may become the sons of God; that when he shall appear we shall be like him, for we shall see him as he is; that we may have this hope; that we may be purified even as he is pure. Amen.

— *Moroni 7:48*

We must remember that personal worship does not allow *us* to produce for *ourselves* the great blessings that the Lord has promised to everyone who diligently seeks him. Rather, personal worship helps us to open our hearts to receiving the gifts that a loving Heavenly Father and Jesus Christ have prepared for each of us. Forgiveness, faith, hope, charity, and a host of other blessings can be ours when we humbly strive to follow the commandments, repent, and do our best to follow the Savior. They are gifts that the Lord gives to those who diligently seek to follow his commandments.

Participating in personal worship helps us to come unto Christ with humility and open hearts. When we follow the Lord in this way, it allows him to change our hearts for us. He can purify us. He can give us the gifts of faith, hope and charity. We have to be willing to receive those gifts. Humble personal worship helps us to open our hearts to those blessings.

Transformations or Transactions?

The aim of all gospel learning and teaching is to deepen our conversion and help us become more like Jesus Christ. For this reason, when we study the gospel, we're not just looking for new information; we want to become a "new creature" (see 2 Corinthians 5:17). This means relying on Christ to change our hearts, our views, our actions, and our very natures.

But the kind of gospel learning that strengthens our faith and leads to the miraculous change of conversion doesn't happen all at once. It extends beyond a classroom into an individual's heart and home. It requires consistent, daily efforts to understand and live the gospel. True conversion requires the influence of the Holy Ghost.

— Come, Follow Me - For Individuals and Families - New Testament

In a recent church meeting, one of the speakers shared an insight on how our personal worship can be used to help us open our hearts to the Holy Ghost. He asked the question: What can you do to make taking the Sacrament transformational instead of transactional? Often, we view the things we do from the perspective of a transaction. When something is a transaction, we view it is an exchange. We do an action to get a reward. For example, we give our time to an employer so they will give us a paycheck. When something is transformational, we view it as an opportunity. We participate to allow it to change us. For example, missionaries choose to serve and show the faith to serve wherever they are called. Serving in this way, most missionaries are profoundly changed by their mission experiences.

Most things in life can be either transactional or transformational depending on our attitudes and intentions. We might do our job only for the paycheck, or we may truly believe that our work helps people. Sometimes we serve others only out of a sense of obligation and not because we truly want to be more like Jesus Christ. We can determine whether an activity will be transactional or transformational by how willing we are to let the activity change us. When we participate in personal worship, we should strive to let those activities be transformational in our lives. Studying the scriptures, honoring the Sabbath, ministering and serving in the temple all have the power to change us in profound ways, *if we let them*. By opening our hearts to the Holy Ghost and seeking to let the Savior change our hearts, we can enable the transformational power of personal worship in our lives.

Experience the strengthening power of daily repentance—of doing and being a little better each day. When we choose to repent, we choose to change! We allow the Savior to transform us into the best version of ourselves. We choose to grow spiritually and receive joy—the joy of redemption in him. When we choose to repent, we choose to become more like Jesus Christ!

The Lord does not expect perfection from us at this point. ... But he does expect us to become increasingly pure. Daily repentance is the pathway to purity.

— *Russell M. Nelson*

As we consistently do our best to draw nearer to the Savior, he will bless us. While perfection is our ultimate goal, it is not an immediate requirement. We can repent daily and try to be a little better. When we repent each day, we will have the power of the Holy Ghost in our lives. We will step by step and line by line grow to become more like Jesus Christ. When we approach this journey with faith and diligence and allow our worship to transform us, we will truly gain the power of the gospel in our lives. This will take time and it will take practice. Lots and lots and *lots* of practice. But when we put forth our best efforts and rely on the Lord, he can transform each of us into the best versions of ourselves. He will bless us with faith. He will bless us with hope. He will help us to become more like him.

We Are at War

We are at war with Satan for the souls of men. The battle lines were drawn in our pre-earth life. Satan and a third of our Father in Heaven's children turned away from His promises of exaltation. Since that time, the adversary's minions have been fighting the faithful who choose the Father's plan.

Satan knows his days are numbered and that time is growing shorter. As crafty and cunning as he is, he will not win. However, his battle for each of our souls rages on.

— Ronald A. Rasband

The Book of Mormon was written by ancient prophets to help us today. One topic that comes up repeatedly in its pages is war. The Book of Mormon contains several accounts of wars between different groups of people. Why would our Heavenly Father need us to know so much about wars from so long ago? Most of us will probably never be called on to fight in a physical battle, but we are all involved in the war for our souls and the souls of those we love.

We can learn a lot about this struggle from the story of the Stripling Warriors. Despite having heard and studied this account often, we can find many lessons which we often overlook when we discuss this inspiring story. For those who might not be familiar with the story of the Stripling Warriors, here is a brief summary.

The Stripling Warriors

The Book of Mormon recounts the history of ancient people on the American continent. We learn about two main groups of people in this history. The Nephites believed in the gospel of Jesus Christ and followed the prophets. The Lamanites did not believe in the gospel or follow the prophets. Throughout the Book of Mormon, the Lamanites were constantly attacking the Nephites to enslave them.

The Stripling Warriors were young men who rallied to the call to fight in a war with the Lamanites. The story of the Stripling Warriors begins with their parents. The parents of the Stripling Warriors were Lamanites. They were among those who had fought for years with the Nephites. Through the efforts of Nephite missionaries, they came to believe in the gospel of Jesus Christ. After going through sore repentance, they made a covenant to never kill again. As a sign of their covenant, they buried their weapons of war deep in the earth. The other Lamanites viewed the faith of the converted Lamanites with disdain and began to slaughter them. Eventually, these new converts fled their homes to join the Nephites. The Nephites welcomed them as new friends and fought to protect them from the other Lamanites from that time forth.

Years later, the Nephites again found themselves in a bitter war with the Lamanites. The war became so intense and the Nephites army's situation so precarious, that the converted Lamanites desired to fight alongside the Nephites who had fought so hard to protect them. It was only at the encouragement of the Lord's prophet that they continued to honor the covenant they had made many years before. The Stripling Warriors were two thousand sons of these converted Lamanites. They were very young when their parents made their covenant and buried their weapons. These young men had not made the covenant of peace. Because they had not entered a covenant to never fight, these young men bravely came to the aid of the Nephite army.

Through the rest of the war, the Stripling Warriors were protected by the power of God. As we read their story, we can learn many lessons that can give us hope in our battles against Satan.

We Are at War with a Relentless Enemy

Satan "is the enemy of righteousness and of those who seek to do the will of God." All day, every day, his only intent and sole purpose are to make the sons and daughters of God miserable like unto himself. ... Understanding the intent of an enemy is vital to effective preparation for possible attacks. Precisely because Captain Moroni knew the intention of the Lamanites, he was prepared to meet them at the time of their coming and was victorious. And that same principle and promise apply to each of us.

— David A. Bednar

We must never forget that Satan is our enemy. He is *always* seeking our destruction. He will *never* do anything that is for our good. Because he is so relentless in seeking our destruction, we too must strive to be valiant and relentless in seeking to follow Jesus Christ. Sometimes we are tempted to think that something isn't *that* bad or that it is acceptable to sin just once. When we are faced with these temptations, we must remember that the devil and his followers are always seeking to find and exploit the small weaknesses in our resolve. We never know when one small thing will lead to a string of consequences.

The stripling warriors "were exceedingly valiant for courage ...; but behold, this was not all—they were ... true at all times in whatsoever thing they were entrusted. Yea, ... they had been taught to keep the commandments of God and to walk uprightly before him." These young men went to war carrying Christlike virtues as weapons against their adversaries. President Thomas S. Monson reminded us that "the call for courage comes constantly to each of us. Every day of our lives

> *courage is needed—not just for the momentous events but more often as we make decisions or respond to circumstances around us."*
>
> *— Joy D. Jones*

We remember the Stripling Warriors for their faith and obedience. They had been taught from a young age that if that had faith and were diligent, they would be protected from harm. They were quick to obey and steadfast in their faith. Because of this, they were protected in their many battles. As we strive to be perfectly obedient, we will be protected from the snares and traps that the devil puts in our path. In scripture, we learn that the Lord works by "small and simple things." The devil knows this and will also try to lead us away from our heavenly home one small step at a time. This is why it is vitally important that we don't rationalize letting evil into our lives. Sometimes we will stumble and struggle, but we should do our best to choose to follow the Lord.

We can take faith in the fact that our Heavenly Father also works by "small and simple things." Just as the devil seeks to lead us away from righteousness one small step at a time, we can also move closer to our Savior one small step at a time. This is why the little things matter. Our path in life is rarely determined by major events, but rather by the seemingly small, but impactful decisions we make daily. We need to seek learning and guidance. When we listen to the teachings of the prophets, both ancient and modern, and strive to follow their council we will learn what our Father in Heaven wants us to do.

The Lord Will Help Us Succeed

Fortifying children to become sin-resistant is a task and a blessing for parents, grandparents, family members, teachers, and leaders. We each bear responsibility to help. However, the Lord has specifically instructed parents to teach their children "to understand the doctrine of repentance, faith in Christ the Son of the living God, and of baptism and the gift of the Holy Ghost" and "to pray, and to walk uprightly before the Lord."

— Joy D. Jones

While we work to learn the gospel and follow the Savior, we are sure to make mistakes. The Lord provided a way for us to overcome these mistakes through the Atonement. We can repent and return to the gospel path whenever we stumble and fall. When we strive each day to do the small and simple things the Lord has asked us to do, he will give us strength to resist Satan's attacks. As we pray, study the scriptures, and seek to serve one another daily, the Lord blesses us with protection and guidance.

If we continually work to follow the example of Jesus Christ and sincerely repent when we come up short, the Savior has the power to change us. Jesus can change our desires to be more like his desires. He gives us the love he has for others. He can sanctify us. These Christlike attributes become a shield and a protection for us against the attacks of the adversary.

We Need to Be Unified

Nothing is so much calculated to lead people to forsake sin as to take them by the hand, and watch over them with tenderness. When persons manifest the least kindness and love to me, O what power it has over my mind, while the opposite course has a tendency to harrow up all the harsh feelings and depress the human mind

— Joseph Smith Jr.

In a great war, no one expects troops to run into a fight one at a time. The power of an army comes from their unity and the support they give one another. The devil has united his forces in their assaults on all that is good and pure. We too must unite and lift and support one another in our fight for what is right.

Often, this may be hard to do. Everyone is in different situations and we all have different opinions and priorities. When we look past our differences and remember we are all children of our Heavenly Father, we can gain a greater desire to lift and strengthen one another. When we stand together, we gain greater strength against the adversary.

We Will All Be Injured

As members of the Church, we are engaged in a mighty conflict. We are at war. We have enlisted in the cause of Christ to fight against Lucifer. … The great war that rages on every side and which unfortunately is resulting in many casualties, some fatal, is no new thing.

— Bruce R. McConkie

The battles the Stripling Warriors fought were bloody, intense scenes of hand-to-hand combat. They were raging battles with a fierce and hateful enemy. This is like the battle we are engaged in with the adversary. This battle is neither distant nor impersonal. It is intense hand-to-hand combat.

The book of Alma tells us what happened to the Stripling Warriors in one of these great battles. It reads, "And it came to pass that there were two hundred, out of my two thousand and sixty, who had fainted because of the loss of blood; nevertheless, according to the goodness of God, and to our great astonishment, and also the joy of our whole army, there was not one soul of them who did perish; yea, and neither was there one soul among them who had not received many wounds." (Alma 57:25) In the battle the Stripling Warriors were *all* injured, with many wounds. We are told that about 10%

of them had "fainted because of the loss of blood." But not a single one of them perished.

In our battles, injuries will occur. What injuries will we receive in these battles? I believe these injuries are the times when we stumble. We are injured when we succumb to the attacks that are thrown at us. They are the times we sin. They are also the times when we experience a trial of faith or a severe heartbreak. For some, they are times of personal doubt and suffering. They are any experience we have that threatens to pull us away from our Savior.

None of us should expect to get through the battles of life without getting injured. We will all have times when we fall short of our true potential. We all have times of weakness when we sin or times of trial when our faith is tested. The miracle of the gospel is that as we repent and turn to the Savior, he can heal us. No matter how deep the wounds, the Savior can heal us, even when we have "fainted because of the loss of blood."

We Need to Go in Search of Each Other

There are so many young people who wander aimlessly and walk the tragic trail of drugs, gangs, immorality, and the whole brood of ills that accompany these things. There are widows who long for friendly voices and that spirit of anxious concern which speaks of love. There are those who were once warm in the faith, but whose faith has grown cold. Many of them wish to come back but do not know quite how to do it. They need friendly hands reaching out to them. With a little effort, many of them can be brought back to feast again at the table of the Lord. My brethren and sisters, I would hope, I would pray, that each of us … would resolve to seek those who need help, who are in desperate and difficult circumstances, and lift them in the spirit of love into the embrace of the Church, where strong hands and loving hearts will warm them, comfort them, sustain them, and put them on the way of happy and productive lives.

— *Gordon B. Hinckley*

How many of those we are charged to care for are lying on the battlefield, fainting with the loss of blood, hoping that someone will come to help them? As Gordon B. Hinckley said, it is our responsibility to seek them out. We can lift them and help them to know that their Father in Heaven loves them. Let them know that you understand how it feels to be wounded in battle. Help them understand the power of repentance and the hope it brings. If we don't seek them out, many of them will perish on the battlefield. We marvel at the miraculous story of the Stripling Warriors, but I wonder how many of them would have perished had their brothers not found them on the battlefield and brought them back to safety.

We must remember that many of our children, parents, friends, family, and others we encounter are out on the battlefield, wounded and bleeding. When the battle was over, the Stripling Warriors went in search of their brothers. They found them. They bound their wounds. They carried them to a place of safety. This is the lesson we need to learn from the Stripling Warriors. This is one of the biggest reasons we have for hope. We can have hope because we can reach out to lift and help those who lay wounded on the battlefield of life. We can have hope when we are wounded on the battlefield of life as others reach out and help us.

So many people around us who need our help. They are lying wounded on the battlefield of life. It is up to us to seek them out and lift them. When we do this, we can help them gain the healing blessings of the Atonement. Doing so will also strengthen us in our battles with the adversary.

The Promise of Hope

When I was fourteen years old, I had an experience that taught me a lot about hope and our Heavenly Father's love. One week our church youth group had plans to go to one of the beaches at the Great Salt Lake for an activity. We were going to have a beach party with sand volleyball, hotdogs and ice cream sandwiches.

After eating and playing volleyball for a minute, some of us decided to play in the super salty water of the Great Salt Lake. The beaches along the Great Salt Lake are different from ocean beaches. Both have sand and salty water, but the beaches at the Great Salt Lake are very shallow and have no waves. You can walk very far out into the water and still barely get wet. The shallowness of the water makes it rather warm and pleasant.

I remember playing with my friends in the water. It was so salty that you could look in the water and see salt crystals forming. You could also see thousands of little brine shrimp in the water. It really was a unique and strange experience. As we were splashing each other and having fun, one of my best friends, Nate, and I decided to try and see how far out in the water we could go before the water got deep. We left the rest of our group and started our expedition out into the lake. We walked and walked into the lake and it very gradually got deeper. Eventually, we were in water that came up to just above our knees.

At this point we decided to see how far out we were. We looked back and saw that we were about 400 yards away from the shore. We stood there feeling somewhat impressed with ourselves when to our dismay we saw everyone packing up and getting loaded into cars to leave. We began running back to shore as quickly as we could but running in knee-deep water is slow and exhausting. We tried to yell for them to wait for us, but we were too far away for anyone to hear us. Desperately running back to the shore, our hearts sank as we watched the last cars in our group pull away.

Eventually, we got back to the shore, found our shoes and looked around confirming that our fears were true – we had been left behind. In today's world, a quick phone call would have summoned one of the leaders back to pick us up, but I grew up in a world without cell phones. We looked and found that the beach parking area had a payphone, but being fourteen and generally unprepared, we didn't have any money and didn't know how to make a collect call. We didn't know what we were going to do. The Great Salt Lake beaches are far from civilization and even gas stations so there was nowhere we could go to ask for help. We stood there for a while and discussed what we could do to get home. Should we try to walk and find a gas station, try to hitch a ride home, or simply sit and wait for someone from our group to return looking for us?

As we stood there processing the weight of our situation and feeling lost, a car pulled up in front of us. It was an older sports car – probably a Trans Am – with rust and obvious signs of age. It was the kind of car that is a piece of garbage that leaks oil and needs constant attention to keep running but is the pride and joy of a high school kid. The driver of the car was one of the young men in our church youth group who had driven to the beach on his own. Nate and I didn't really know him, but we knew he was in our youth group. He offered to give us a ride home and given that we literally had no other options, we gladly accepted. The inside of his car was exactly what you might expect. It was full of loud music and garbage.

I don't remember much about the ride home except feeling like it was taking *forever*. Despite our desires to get home as quickly as possible our newfound friend was in no hurry. He needed gas, so we stopped at a 7-Eleven. He bought us Big Gulps. He bought oil and put it in the car. And in all of this, he took his time. I am sure in hindsight that he probably got us home pretty quickly but given my anxiety at the time it did not feel that way.

Eventually, we did make it home almost two hours after everyone else had returned. I remember walking into my house repentant with an empty Big Gulp cup in my hand. As you might expect, my parents and our church leaders had been very worried. They had been trying to figure out where we were with the fevered anxiety that possibly only parents of a lost child know. I had been worried that I would be in huge trouble when I got home, but after recounting the story of my evening I was greeted with my parents' love and relief that I was finally home safe and sound.

I don't know that Nate and I ever talked much with the young man who got us home that night. He moved away shortly after this experience. As I have reflected on that experience though, I have come to see him as a blessing from the Lord. That night our Heavenly Father knew we needed help and he sent help our way. It wasn't the help we would have chosen for ourselves, but it was the help we needed to get back home.

Just like me and my friend Nate in this story, we all have times when we feel lost and alone. Times when we have wandered out into deep water away from the safety provided by those who love us. Times when we doubt our abilities and despair that we will not be successful. You may have experienced being left behind like I did that night, or you may have only felt lost in a more spir-itual sense. Either way, if you have felt the despair and fear that accompanies such experiences, you are not alone.

Throughout this book we have discussed the stories of many people who have also experienced such feel-ings of hopelessness. In the stories of Nephi, Laman, Lemuel, the Brother of Jared, the Stripling Warriors, me and Nate at the Great Salt Lake and countless others we see people who were faced with seemingly insurmountable obstacles that challenged their faith and confidence. We have also seen how the Lord always provides the help to those in need when they trust him. We can have hope because our Heavenly Father loves us and will *always* provide the help we need. We just need to trust him and accept the help he provides.

For each and every one of us, the promise of the gospel of Jesus Christ is the promise of hope. We are all imperfect. We are all a big stucco Buddha sitting under a tin shed feeling unnoticed, unappreciated and unimportant. But inside each of us is a stunning golden Buddha. A wonderful, powerful and valuable inner self. While we may not clearly see that now, we can bit by bit and step by step do the work we need to do to become that heavenly version of ourselves. We do not need to experience an immediate transformation. We do not need to move mountains today. But we do need to take consistent, small steps in the right direction. We need to continue each day to strive to become more like our Savior. We can progress daily by taking small steps to improve. Because we can progress gradually, each of us can succeed in our efforts to become more like our Savior. This is the promise and reason for hope.

Our Heavenly Father loves each of us. He loves every person you will ever see. And he loves *you*. He knows your name. He knows you have the potential inside you to become like him. He did not send us into mortality just to watch us fail. He sent us here to allow us to succeed. We can trust that he knows what he is doing and that we can all receive the blessings of exaltation that he has prepared for us. The Atonement doesn't apply to everyone except you. The blessings of the Atonement and the opportunity to overcome our sins and be perfected in Christ are available to *everyone* and that includes you and me. We can trust that our Heavenly Father knows what he is doing in sending us into this life and that he will do all he can to ensure we return to him.

As we cultivate this trust in our Heavenly Father and our Savior, Jesus Christ, we will begin to see the wonderful blessings they have prepared for each of us. We can gain a clear vision of the men and women we can become with the Lord's help. Like a map, this vision of our future will direct us and give us perspective as we valiantly work to overcome the challenges we face. We will all have trials and obstacles to overcome in our journey, but we can trust in the Lord's promises. We can have faith that he is leading us back to our heavenly home with him.

As we work to follow the Lord each day, we will make consistent progress back to him. A great life is made from great years. Great years are made from great months. And great months are made from great days. Just as one builds a house one brick at a time, we build our life one day at a time. By doing our best to build great days, we can know that we are building the life we really want. When we do our best to live the gospel daily, we can rely on our hope of obtaining the wonderful future blessings we desire.

Along our journey, there will be days that don't turn out how we want. We will stumble and fall. We will make mistakes as we work to overcome our weaknesses and draw nearer to the Lord. When this happens, we can repent and try again. The Atonement gives us the opportunity to try again no matter how many times it takes. When we repent and try again each time we fail, we will eventually become like our Savior. We can overcome our weaknesses. We can improve little by little until we are truly like Jesus Christ. He will help us each step of the way.

The journey of this life is long. It will take time to learn and grow. The Lord has given us opportunities to draw near to him through personal worship that can help us feel the Holy Spirit. When we engage in sincere personal worship, the Lord will guide us through personal revelation. He will help us know what we need to do to draw nearer to him. He will show us the way and he will help us overcome our weaknesses and every obstacle and challenge we encounter.

I do not know why we have the many trials that we have, but it is my personal feeling that the reward is so great, so eternal and everlasting, so joyful and beyond our understanding that in that day of reward, we may feel to say to our merciful, loving father, "Was that all that was required?" I believe that if we could daily remember and recognize the depth of that love our Heavenly Father and our Savior have for us, we would be willing to do anything to be back in Their presence again, surrounded by Their love eternally. What will it matter what we suffered here if, in the end, those trials are the very things which qualify us for eternal life and exaltation in the kingdom of God with our father and Savior?

— Linda S. Reeves

Despite the opposition and challenges we will encounter; we can trust that the Lord loves us and wants us to return to him. Satan knows that heaven is within reach for each of us, and he will do all he can to keep us from getting there. But the Lord is on our side. The Lord has already gained victory over death and provided us a way to repent and be forgiven of our sins and weaknesses through the Atonement. The Savior's victory in the war for the souls of me and women is assured. All we have to do to be victorious is to keep moving forward and follow the Lord. We are not alone in this battle. The Lord is on our side and he allows us to lift and help each other. Our Heavenly Father and Jesus Christ love each of us. They know who you are, and they know your fears, challenges, weaknesses and trials. They know all this and still love you more than you can comprehend, and they will do all they can to help you return home. Together we cannot lose and that may be the biggest reason we have for hope.

Acknowledgements

This book would not be possible without the help of so many people. I want to start by expressing my gratitude to the many teachers, guides, mentors and friends who have helped me become the person I am today. I am forever thankful to my Heavenly Father and Jesus Christ for the constant stream of blessings that I have received in my life. I am thankful to my wife, Trisha, for her constant love and support. I am thankful for my four wonderful children Logan, Maddy, Aiden, and Colin. They are each unique and amazing. They constantly push me to be a better person and watching them succeed is one of my greatest joys in life. I am thankful to my parents, Mike & Launa, for their constant love and encouragement. I am thankful to my brother and sister and my many brothers and sisters in-law and my father and mother in-law. Your love and support and friendship are something I value beyond measure. I am grateful to my many friends and neighbors that have made life a wonderful adventure for me and my family.

I am also grateful for the many authors and teachers who have written inspiring and thought-provoking books that have helped me learn and grow in my journey of life. I am especially thankful for Dr. Benjamin Hardy and my mentoring group for their encouragement as I have worked on this book and many other life goals.

Acknowledgements

Their guidance and support has helped me achieve goals I had previously only hoped for.

I am grateful for everyone who helped me in any way as I have worked on this book. I am thankful for those who have given feedback and taken time to read my book and offer suggestions and feedback. You are all awesome!

Lastly, I am thankful to every one of you who have taken the time to read my book. My only hope is that this book helps you gain more hope in your life. Never forget that we all have reason to hope.

About the Author

Dave Haslam is a husband and father of four wonderful children. He loves spending time with his family and seeing his wife and children grow and do amazing things. He is constantly impressed by the amazing things they do. He loves to go on adventures and spend time in the mountains with his family.

Dave Haslam is a member of the Church of Jesus Christ of Latter-Day Saints, and served a church mission in Nagoya, Japan. He loves to learn and tries to learn something new every day. He gets super excited when he discovers a new insight that helps him understand things from a different perspective and he loves to share the things he learns with others.

Dave writes the blog *Foundations for Eternity* on www.dmhaslam.com. He enjoys the opportunity to connect with his readers and sincerely hopes to be able to help encourage people on their personal journeys of faith.

Dave lives with his wife, four kids and two dogs in Bluffdale, UT.

You can connect with Dave Haslam in several ways:

The author website: www.dmhaslam.com

Email: dmhaslam@gmail.com

Instagram: @dave.haslam